SEEKING

Biblical Answers to Life's Toughest Questions

OBED OLIVARRÍA

metamorphosis
PUBLISHERS

Cover design by Obed Olivarría

Typeset and inside design by Obed Olivarría

Library of Congress Control Number: 2024923596

ISBN (print edition): 979-8-9913504-2-6

ISBN (eBook edition): 979-8-9913504-3-3

First Edition: August 2025

Metamorphosis Publishers.

Santa Ana, California.

For information contact:

http://www.obedolivarria.com

Contents

Introduction

The Journey of Seeking

I N OUR JOURNEY THROUGH life, we often encounter tough questions that can leave us feeling lost and confused. In times of suffering and pain, uncertainty about our purpose and calling, struggles with faith and doubt, and challenges to our mental health and wellbeing, it's easy to feel lost and overwhelmed.

However, in seeking, we are engaging in an act of faith, challenging as it may be, that propels us forward through the shifting sands of our existence towards a horizon filled with the promise of understanding, or at the very le

ast, a sense of peace with the mysteries that elude us. And seeking biblical answers to life's toughest questions is not just about finding quick fixes or simple solutions. It is about developing a deeper understanding of God's plan for our lives and learning to trust in His timing and His ways.

By approaching our struggles with faith and humility, we can open ourselves up to the transformative power of God's Word and allow it to shape our thoughts, actions, and beliefs. And by grounding ourselves in the timeless truths of Scripture, we can find peace amid chaos, hope in the face of despair, and strength in times of weakness.

So, navigating this journey of seeking with faith is not about finding straightforward answers or quick solutions. Rather, it is about anchoring ourselves in beliefs that give our lives meaning, embracing the lessons that challenge and teach us, and moving forward with a sense of purpose, dignity, clarity, understanding, and hope. It requires courage, perseverance, and an unwavering trust in the journey itself.

In the end, the journey of seeking itself transforms us. It molds our character, connects us more profoundly with the world, and deepens our understanding of the divine. Especially when we find the answers and we apply them in our daily lives!

Purpose of the Book

This book, *Seeking Biblical Answers to Life's Toughest Questions*, serves as a reminder of the importance of seeking wisdom and guidance from the Bible to navigate these difficult times and for seeking answers. The Word of God is our ultimate source of truth and comfort, offering us hope and direction in times of uncertainty.

The purpose of *Seeking Biblical Answers to Life's Toughest Questions* is to provide a comprehensive overview of how biblical wisdom can answer the most pressing questions we face in life. The Bible is not just a book of stories and teachings, but a living and powerful tool that can provide us with the strength and clarity we need to navigate life; and by delving into the Bible, we can find solace, guidance, and comfort in the face of adversity. Through the stories of biblical figures who have grappled with similar challenges, we learn we are not alone in our struggles and that there is hope to be found in God's promises.

In the chapters that follow, we will explore the themes of mercy, joy, fulfillment, compassion, wisdom, freedom, truth, peace, rest, love, and the Divine, among others, in a world that often contradicts the very essence of these values. Each chapter, a step further into the depths of human experience and desire, beckons us to continue on our quest, ever seeking, ever journeying towards that which is eternal, unchanging, and true.

Foundation for Seeking

Three Bible verses inspired this writing—Jeremiah 29:13, Matthew 7:7, and Amos 5:17. First, in the journey of seeking biblical answers to life's toughest questions, we must first understand the importance of seeking with all our hearts, as emphasized in Jeremiah 29:13. This verse reminds us that true seeking requires wholehearted commitment and dedication. It is not a passive pursuit, but an active and intentional effort to seek God's wisdom and guidance in all aspects of our lives. When we seek with all our hearts, we open ourselves up to experiencing the fullness of God's presence and the richness of His truth.

Second, Matthew 7:7 offers us a powerful promise: when we seek, we will find. This verse serves as a reminder that God is faithful to those who diligently seek Him. It encourages us to persevere in our seeking, knowing that God will not withhold His wisdom and guidance from those who earnestly desire it. As we continue to seek God with persistence and faith, we can trust in His promise to reveal Himself to us and guide us in the paths of righteousness.

And last, Amos 5:17 reminds us of the importance of seeking good and God's presence in our lives. This verse speaks to the need for us to prioritize seeking God's righteousness and goodness above all else. When we seek after God's presence and align our lives with His will, we invite His blessings and favor into our lives. By seeking good and God, we cultivate a deeper relationship with Him and experience the transformative power of His love and grace.

So, as Christian readers seeking biblical answers to life's toughest questions, let these verses inspire and guide us,

It's like a divine GPS: Jeremiah 29:13 guarantees, "You will seek me and find me when you seek me with all your heart." And Matthew 7:7 is basically the universe's best-kept secret: "Ask and it will be given to you; seek and you will find; knock and the door will be opened to you."

Invitation to Seek

Upon reading these verses, it sounds like God is inviting us to a cosmic scavenger hunt, doesn't it? So, let us accept the invitation and commit ourselves to seeking with all our heart, trusting in the promise of finding when we seek, and prioritizing seeking good and God's in all that we do. May these verses serve as a reminder of the importance of seeking God's wisdom, guidance, and presence in our lives, and may they inspire us to pursue a deeper relationship with Him each day.

Remember that in seeking, we embark on a journey that is both profoundly personal and universally shared. It is a journey that does not promise simple answers, but offers the possibility of finding purpose, resilience, and a deeper connection to the divine amidst the labyrinth of human experience. So, I invite you to partake in the great human endeavor of seeking light in the darkness. Happy seeking!

May this book serve as a beacon of light and a source of inspiration for all who seek to deepen their faith, find answers to life's toughest questions, and grow closer to God. Let us embark on this journey together, with open hearts and minds, as we seek the wisdom and guidance of the Bible to navigate the challenges of life.

Chapter 1

Seeking Meaning in a Drifting World

Introduction: The quest for purpose in a seemingly aimless world

IN A WORLD FILLED with chaos and uncertainty, it is easy to feel lost and uncertain about our direction. Many of us often grapple with the question of purpose in a seemingly aimless world. We yearn for a sense of meaning and fulfillment, and we strive to find our purpose and calling, but struggle to find it in our daily struggles and challenges.

As humans, in our relentless pursuit for meaning, we have journeyed through various aspects of life in search of something greater, something beyond the immediate and tangible. Often, this journey takes us through realms of thought and belief that border the metaphysical, challenging our perceptions and beliefs about life, death, and what lies beyond. But, as Salomon said, it's all meaningless.

It often feels like we are in a hamster wheel—round and round we go, getting nowhere. Many times, we chase after career success, personal achievements, and material possessions, only to end up feeling like a deflated balloon at the end of a party.

It is in times like these that we must turn to the ultimate guide—the Bible—to find true meaning in life and ensure that we don't just drift through life like a rubber ducky in a kiddie pool. Even though seeking biblical answers is not always easy, it is a journey worth embarking on.

This is because, as we delve into the Scriptures, we remember of God's promises and his unwavering love for us. His promises reassure us we are not alone in our search for purpose and direction, for God has a plan for every one of us. The Bible teaches us God uniquely created us for a specific purpose.

By seeking His guidance and following His will, we can discover our unique gifts and talents and use them to glorify Him and serve others, and we can find our true calling and live a life of fulfillment and purpose in this world. By seeking Him with all our hearts, we can discover the gifts and talents He has given us and use them to fulfill the purpose He has set before us. Trust in God's timing and guidance, and He will lead you to a life filled with purpose and meaning.

Biblical Context: Ecclesiastes 3:1-8: A time for everything; Jeremiah 29:11: Plans for a future and hope

The Bible has a lot to say about purpose and meaning. Ecclesiastes 3:1-8 reminds us that there is a time for everything in life and a season for every activity under the heavens—a time to laugh, a time to cry, a time to dance, and even a time to mourn. This isn't just poetic wisdom; it's a divine planner showing that life isn't a chaotic mess, but a carefully orchestrated plan. This passage speaks to the ebb and flow of life's seasons, emphasizing that there is a purpose for every moment we experience.

It's like a cosmic schedule that God has set for us, reminding us that life is full of difficulties, twists, and turns. So next time you find yourself in a tough spot, just remember that this too shall pass—probably right after you've finished that pint of ice cream. So, whether we are facing times of joy or times of sorrow, we can take comfort in knowing that God has ordained each season for a reason. This biblical context also serves as a powerful reminder that we are not alone in our journey through life, and that God is with us every step of the way.

Jeremiah 29:11 assures us God has plans for us—plans to prosper us, not to harm us, plans to give us hope and a future. It's like having a GPS for life, minus the annoying "recalculating" every time we mess up. This passage offers a message of hope and assurance for the future. In times of uncertainty and doubt, we can turn to this promise as a source of strength and encouragement. God's plans may not always align with our own; but hey, His plans are way better, anyway!

So, when life throws you a curveball, just trust that God's got your back and His plans are way cooler than yours. Who knows, maybe His plan involves you becoming a famous llama whisperer—stranger things have happened! Ultimately, trust that God's plans for us are far greater than we could ever imagine, and we can trust in His faithfulness to guide us towards a future filled with hope and purpose.

As Christian readers seeking biblical answers to life's toughest questions, we can find solace in the truths revealed in Ecclesiastes 3:1-8 and Jeremiah 29:11. These passages remind us that our lives are in God's hands, and that He has a perfect plan for every one of us. Even in suffering and pain, we can hold on to the promise that there is a time for everything, and that God's plans for us are good.

When we are wrestling with questions of purpose and calling, we can find guidance in these verses. They remind us that God has a specific plan for our lives, and that He will lead us towards fulfilling our unique purpose. In times of doubt and uncertainty, we can trust in God's promises to provide us with hope and direction.

Ultimately, these passages remind us that God is sovereign over all things, and that by holding onto these promises, we can find peace and strength in life's challenges, knowing that God plans for us to have a hope filled future.

Finding Personal Purpose

We are called to seek God's purpose for our lives. Through prayer and reflection, we can uncover the unique gifts and talents that God has blessed us with. By spending time in quiet contemplation and seeking guidance from the Holy Spirit, we discover the path God set before us. It is through this process of seeking God's will that we can find fulfillment and meaning in our lives. And finding personal meaning begins with understanding that we are part of a larger story—God's story. Our lives have purpose because a purposeful God created us. Here are some practical steps to discovering your purpose:

1. **Seek God's Guidance:** Spend time in prayer and ask God to reveal His plans for your life. Think of it as a divine brainstorming session.

2. **Reflect on Your Gifts and Passions:** Consider what talents and interests God has given you. These can be indicators of your purpose. Remember, you're not just a random collection of quirks and skills—God doesn't make junk!

3. **Serve Others:** Often, we find meaning when we focus on helping others rather than just ourselves. It's amazing how a little less "me" can lead to a lot more fulfillment.

Biblical Examples

The stories of Joseph and Esther are powerful examples of individuals who discovered their God-given purpose and found meaning in their lives. These stories remind us that God can use even the most unlikely circumstances to fulfill His plans and purposes in our lives. Joseph went from being a prisoner to the second most powerful man in Egypt, all because he trusted in God's plan.

And Esther risked her life to save her people, proving that sometimes our purpose is bigger than ourselves. By studying the lives of these biblical characters, we can draw inspiration and guidance for our own journey of discovering purpose and calling.

- **Joseph:** Despite facing betrayal and hardship, and then being sold into slavery by his own brothers (talk about family drama!), Joseph remained faithful to God. Before rising to a position of great influence in Egypt, he ended up in prison for a crime he didn't commit. But even there, he kept his cool and trusted in God's plan. Eventually, Joseph found his purpose in saving Egypt and his family from famine (Genesis 37-50). It's like a rags-to-riches story with a divine twist.

- **Esther:** As a young Jewish woman who eventually became queen, Esther risked her life to save her people, recognizing that she was in her position "for such a time as this" (Esther 4:14) to fulfill the purpose that God had for her. Imagine being in a beauty pageant and suddenly finding out you're the only one who can save your entire nation. Talk about pressure! Yet Esther courageously and gracefully embraced her purpose, and she saved an entire nation.

Practical Application

To apply these principles, try the following exercises:

1. **Journaling:** Write about your prayers, reflections, and any insights you receive about your purpose. It's like a diary, but with more divine direction and fewer high school crushes.

2. **Volunteering:** Get involved in activities that serve others. This can help clarify what you are passionate about. Plus, it's a great way to meet new people and

maybe even find your own "Joseph" or "Esther" story.

3. **Seek Mentorship:** Find a mentor who can provide guidance and wisdom as you seek to understand your purpose. Think of them as your personal Yoda, but with fewer riddles and more practical advice.

Conclusion

In a drifting world, we can find meaning by remembering that God has a unique plan and purpose for each of us. By understanding that we are part of His larger story, using our gifts and passions, and serving others, we can discover the purpose He has for us. By studying the stories of biblical characters like Joseph and Esther, we can glean wisdom and inspiration for our own journey of faith. Remember Jeremiah 29:13: "You will seek Me and find Me when you seek Me with all your heart." So, stop drifting like a lost balloon and start soaring with purpose. After all, God's got your back (and your front, and your sides, too). So, strive to live out your purpose with courage and conviction, knowing that God is always with you, guiding and directing our steps.

Take some time each day to connect with God through prayer and meditation. Ask Him to reveal His plan for your life and listen closely to His gentle whispers. You never know, you might just stumble upon your calling while brushing your teeth or waiting in line at the grocery store. And sure, trusting God's plan for your life can be challenging, especially when we face uncertainty or adversity, or when things don't go as planned.

But remember, He's the ultimate party planner, and He knows exactly what He's doing. God is in control and has a perfect plan for each of us. By placing our trust in Him and surrendering our will to His, we can find peace and assurance in knowing that He is working all things for our good. Trusting in God's plan requires faith and patience, but the rewards of following His guidance are immeasurable.

So, sit back, relax, and trust that His plan for your life is far better than anything you could ever imagine. Discovering your God-given purpose and finding a personal calling is no easy feat. But with a prayer, reflection, and trust in God's plan, you'll be well on your way to living a purpose-driven life. So, go forth with confidence, knowing that God's got your back, and He's leading you towards something truly amazing.

Chapter 2

Seeking Justice in an Unfair World

Introduction: The desire for fairness in a world full of injustice

J USTICE IS A CONCEPT deeply ingrained in us, like our collective love for free samples at the grocery store. We all crave fairness and righteousness, yet the world often feels like a rigged carnival game—no matter how hard we try, the giant teddy bear remains just out of reach. Daily, we face the harsh reality of living in a world that is plagued by injustice and unfairness. It's disheartening to see the innocent suffer while the wicked prosper, and to witness the oppression of the marginalized and vulnerable. In times like these, it is natural to question why God allows such injustices to exist and to wonder if there is any hope for a fair and just world.

Once again, in our search for answers on how can pursue justice, even when the world seems inherently unjust, we turn to the ultimate source of wisdom and truth—the Bible. Throughout its pages, we find stories of struggle, suffering, and injustice, but we also find hope, redemption, and justice. The Bible teaches us that God is a God of justice, and that He cares deeply about the oppressed and marginalized. It reminds us that ultimately, God will right all wrongs and bring about true justice for all. And we can trust that God is just because He has shown us time and time again in His Word that He is a fair and righteous judge.

When we engage in social justice from a biblical perspective, we are following in the footsteps of Jesus, Who stood up for the oppressed and marginalized. It is not enough to believe in God's justice. We must also act upon it by advocating for those who cannot advocate for themselves. This means standing up against injustice, speaking out against inequality, and actively working towards a more just society.

Biblical Context: Micah 6:8: Acting justly, loving mercy, walking humbly; Psalm 82:3-4: Defending the weak and fatherless

The Bible provides us with timeless wisdom and guidance. In Micah 6:8, we are called to be agents of change in a world that is broken and unjust. We are called to act justly, seek justice, love mercy, and walk humbly with our God. Now, I don't know about you, but sometimes I struggle to even walk humbly after a big meal, let alone with God by my side. But hey, baby steps, right? However, this isn't just a feel-good bumper sticker; it's a divine mandate. By aligning ourselves with God's purposes and calling, we can be a light in the darkness and a voice for the voiceless. When we live out our purpose with passion and conviction, we can make a meaningful impact on the world and bring about positive change.

These words serve as a powerful reminder of how we are called to live our lives. Acting just means standing up for what is right, even when it is difficult. Loving mercy involves showing compassion and forgiveness to others, just as God has shown us mercy. And walking humbly reminds us to approach our relationship with God with humility and reverence.

Similarly, Psalm 82:3-4 further emphasizes the importance of defending the weak and fatherless and urges us to "Defend the weak and the fatherless; uphold the cause of the poor and the oppressed. Rescue the weak and the needy deliver them from the hand of the wicked." This verse is like the ultimate call to action for all of us to stand up for those who are most vulnerable in our society. It's like God is saying, "Hey, don't just sit there scrolling through Instagram. Get out there and make a difference!"

And let's be real, defending the weak and fatherless isn't always easy. Sometimes it means getting out of our comfort zones and putting ourselves in uncomfortable situations. But hey, Jesus didn't come to Earth to hang out in His comfort zone, did He? So, we are called to be a voice for the voiceless and to stand up for those who are vulnerable and marginalized. We are called to be advocates for justice and compassion in our world. Essentially, we're being told to be superheroes, minus the capes (but if you want to wear one, no judgment here). By defending the weak and fatherless, we are living out our faith in a tangible and impactful way.

As we navigate through the complexities of life, it's easy to lose sight of our calling as Christians. However, when we reflect on these powerful verses, they remind us of the importance of living out our faith in our daily lives. Whenever we struggle with issues of injustice, the words of Micah 6:8 and Psalm 82:3-4 offer us hope and inspiration.

Let these words encourage us to act justly, love mercy, and walk humbly with our God. Inspire us to defend the weak and fatherless, and to be a beacon of light and love in a world that is often dark and broken. May these verses serve as a reminder of our calling. And if you ever feel you're struggling to live up to these ideals, just remember that even the disciples probably had their off days. We're all a work in progress, but with God by our side, we can keep striving to be the best versions of ourselves.

Pursuing Biblical Justice

Justice in the biblical sense involves more than fairness; it encompasses righteousness, mercy, and advocacy for the vulnerable. In our journey of seeking justice, we must first start by trusting that God is just. As a Christian, we believe God is fair and righteous in all His ways, even when we may not understand His ways. This trust in His justice allows us to navigate through life's challenges with a sense of peace and assurance that He is always working for our good. Here's how we can pursue justice:

1. **Seek God's Wisdom:** Pray for guidance in understanding and enacting justice. Think of it as downloading divine updates for your moral compass.

2. **Stand Up for the Oppressed:** Engaging in social justice from a biblical perspective is another practical application of our faith. Use your voice and resources to defend those who cannot defend themselves. Channel your inner Moses and speak truth to power.

3. **Live Righteously:** Strive to align your actions with God's standards of justice and righteousness. It's like following a heavenly user manual for life.

Biblical Examples

Looking at examples of biblical justice, we can draw inspiration and guidance from many characters. In fact, the Bible describes many with justice warriors—or superheroes—who stood up against unfairness and made a difference. Moses, known for leading the Israelites out of slavery in Egypt, stood up against the oppressive Pharaoh and fought for the freedom of his people. God heard the cries of His people and raised up Moses to be their deliverer. Through a series of miraculous events, God showed His justice by freeing the Israelites from oppression and leading them to the promised land.

Nehemiah, likewise, rebuilt the walls of Jerusalem and restored justice and order in the land. Despite facing opposition and threats, Nehemiah remained steadfast in his faith and determination to see justice done. Through prayer, perseverance, and hard work, Nehemiah could restore justice and order to the city. These stories remind us of the power of faith and action in bringing about justice and righteousness into the world.

- **Moses:** Imagine living in ancient Egypt and witnessing systemic oppression daily. That was Moses's reality. Despite his initial reluctance and some serious self-doubt (remember the burning bush incident?), Moses led the Israelites out of Egyptian slavery. He confronted Pharaoh with nothing but his faith and a staff, demonstrating that even the mightiest empires can't withstand divine justice (Exodus 3-14). Moses didn't just talk about justice; he lived through it, leading an entire nation to freedom.

- **Nehemiah:** Nehemiah had a pretty cushy job as the cupbearer to the Persian king. But when he heard about the crumbling walls of Jerusalem and the plight of his people, he traded his comfortable position for a hard hat, boots, and a vision of justice. He rallied the people to rebuild the walls and instituted reforms to ensure fairness and justice among them (Nehemiah 5). Nehemiah showed seeking justice often means getting into the thick of it and doing it yourself.

Practical Application

Active participation in movements focused on justice, environmental conservation, and human rights can galvanize collective action and inspire widespread change. To apply these principles, try the following exercises:

1. **Advocacy:** Engage in efforts to support social justice causes, such as volunteering with organizations that fight for human rights. Consider it your superhero

training program.

2. **Community Involvement:** Contribute to local government or community groups that work towards justice and equity. Be the change you want to see, even if it starts with attending a town hall meeting.

3. **Educate Yourself:** Learn about issues of injustice and ways to address them biblically. Knowledge is power, and in this case, it's also a way to equip yourself for the fight against injustice.

Conclusion

In a world rife with injustice, we are called to be instruments of God's justice. We are called to advocate for the marginalized, oppressed, and vulnerable in society. This means standing up for those who cannot stand up for themselves, speaking out against injustice, and working towards a more reasonable and compassionate world. By aligning our actions with biblical principles of justice, we can make a tangible difference in the lives of those who are suffering. And by seeking God's wisdom, standing up for the oppressed, and living righteously, we can make a meaningful impact.

So, let's put on our metaphorical (or literal) capes and take a stand. Let us go forth with humility and determination, knowing that God's justice will always prevail in the end. After all, even in an unfair world, we have the power to make a difference, one act of justice at a time.

We trust God is just and actively engaging in social justice from a biblical perspective. By following the examples of Moses and Nehemiah, we can see that justice is not just a concept, but a calling for all believers. Let us remember that justice is a foundational principle of our faith.

By trusting in God's own justice, engaging in social justice from a biblical perspective, and learning from the examples of biblical justice, we can find hope, inspiration, and direction in our quest for answers. May we empower ourselves to be agents of change and transformation in a world that desperately needs God's justice and love.

Chapter 3

Seeking Mercy in a Cruel World

Introduction: The need for mercy amid cruelty

T HE WORLD CAN OFTEN seem harsh and unforgiving, like that one grocery store cashier who always finds and publicly comment on your most embarrassing purchase. In such an environment, finding mercy can feel like trying to hug a cactus—challenging and potentially painful. In fact, the world is so filled with cruelty and suffering that it's easy to lose sight of the importance of showing mercy and compassion to those around us. In the Bible, we are called to embrace and emulate the love and mercy of Jesus Christ in all that we do, and also to extend mercy, reflecting God's compassion and love, even when the world seems determined to be cruel.

The Bible is full of teachings on the importance of mercy and compassion. In Matthew 5:7, Jesus tells us, "Blessed are the merciful, for they will be shown mercy." This verse reminds us it is through showing mercy to others that we will receive mercy in return. As we strive to navigate the challenges of life, we must remember it is through acts of kindness and compassion that we can make a difference in the lives of those around us. When faced with cruelty and suffering, it's easy to become resentful.

However, as Christians, we must remember it is through showing mercy that we can overcome the darkness that surrounds us. In Romans 12:21, the verse reminds us to "not be overcome by evil, but overcome evil with good." This powerful message serves as a reminder that it is through acts of mercy and kindness that we can combat the cruelty and suffering that exists in the world.

Last, as we navigate life's toughest questions, let us also remember the words of Colossians 3:12, which urges us to "clothe ourselves with compassion, kindness, humility, gentleness, and patience." By embodying these qualities and showing mercy to others, we can bring light and hope to a world that is often filled with darkness and despair.

Biblical Context: Matthew 5:7: Blessed are the merciful; Luke 6:36: Being merciful as God is merciful

In the Sermon on the Mount found in Matthew, Jesus proclaims, "Blessed are the merciful, for they will be shown mercy." This powerful statement isn't just a heavenly barter system; it's a way of life that transforms us and those around us. It reminds us of the importance of showing compassion and kindness to others. Now, I don't know about you, but I sure could use a healthy dose of mercy now and then.

It's like a spiritual boomerang—the more mercy we show to others, the more mercy comes back to us. We are called to embody the spirit of mercy in our daily lives, extending grace and forgiveness to those in need. By practicing mercy, we not only reflect the love of God, but also experience His abundant blessings in return. So, let's get out there and start spreading that mercy around like confetti at a birthday party.

Similarly, in Luke, Jesus urges his followers to "Be merciful, just as your Father is merciful." This statement is a divine call to follow the ultimate example of mercy; and Who better to emulate than the expert Himself? I don't know about you, but being as merciful as God sounds like a pretty tall order. I mean, have you seen how patient and forgiving He is with us humans? It's like trying to keep up with a marathon runner when you can barely make it up a flight of stairs without getting winded.

But this commandment challenges us to emulate the unconditional love and compassion of God in our interactions with others. As we strive to be as merciful as our Heavenly Father, we can bring light and hope to a world filled with darkness and despair. Through acts of kindness and understanding, we have the power to transform lives and spread God's love to those in need.

Jesus's teachings often touch on the concept of mercy, and the theme recurs throughout the Bible. From the parable of the Good Samaritan to the forgiveness of the woman caught in adultery, Jesus consistently shows the importance of showing compassion and forgiveness to others. As a Christian, we are called to follow in His footsteps and extend mercy to all, regardless of their past mistakes or shortcomings. Because when we choose to be merciful, we not only reflect the character of God, but also experience His transformative power in our own lives.

Through acts of mercy, we can heal broken relationships, bring comfort to the hurting, and offer hope to the despairing. As we seek to be merciful, as God is merciful, we open ourselves up to a deeper understanding of His love and grace, leading us closer to our ultimate purpose and calling as His children.

In the mandate to be merciful, thankfully, we have the ultimate role model in God Himself, showing us how to extend grace and compassion to others, even when they don't deserve it. It's like having a heavenly cheerleader rooting for us every step of the way, reminding us that mercy is not just an option—it's a calling. Being merciful is not just a suggestion—it's a commandment. Let's be a shining beacon of God's love and compassion in a world that desperately needs it. And who knows, maybe along the way, we'll receive a little extra dose of mercy ourselves. After all, we could all use a little more mercy in our lives. Am I right?

Embracing Mercy

The call to be merciful is a central theme in the teachings of Jesus and a foundational principle of the Christian faith. By embodying the spirit of mercy in our daily lives, we can make a profound impact on the world and experience the fullness of God's blessings. As we strive to be merciful like Jesus, may we extend grace and forgiveness to all, reflecting the love and compassion of Christ to a world in need. In our daily lives, it's easy to get caught up in the hustle and bustle of the world.

However, we are called to embrace and extend mercy to those around us. This means showing compassion and forgiveness to others, even when it may be difficult. By practicing mercy in our daily interactions, we can reflect God's own mercy on us and spread His love to those in need.

1. **Understand God's Mercy:** Recognize the depth of God's mercy towards us, which enables us to extend mercy to others. Picture it like this: If God's mercy were a pie, it would be an infinite, never-ending supply of your favorite flavor. And guess what? We're encouraged to share slices with everyone.

2. **Forgive Freely:** Practice forgiveness, even when it's difficult. Think of it as

emotional decluttering—letting go of grudges can free up space for more joy and peace.

3. **Show Compassion:** Actively look for ways to help those in need. It's like being a kindness detective, always on the lookout for opportunities to make someone's day better.

Biblical Examples

Throughout the Bible, we find countless rich stories of mercy that serve as powerful examples for us to follow and that can inspire us to act with compassion and love. These stories of mercy in the Bible are not only inspiring but also serve as great examples for us to follow. One of the most well-known parables is that of the Good Samaritan, who showed kindness and mercy to a stranger in need. Here we have a man who showed mercy to a stranger in need, despite their differences. It reminds us we are called to show mercy to all, no matter their background or beliefs.

And also, Jesus himself exhibited incredible mercy and forgiveness, even in the face of betrayal and suffering. Despite our many shortcomings, He forgave us and offered us salvation. So, the next time you find it hard to show mercy, just think of these powerful stories from the Bible. These stories remind us of the importance of extending mercy to others, regardless of their background or circumstances.

- **The Good Samaritan:** This classic tale (Luke 10:25-37) involves a man who, despite being from a group despised by the injured man's people, stops to help a stranger beaten and left for dead. The Good Samaritan not only tends to the man's wounds but also ensures an inn cares for him, covering the expenses. This story shows that mercy knows no boundaries and is always in season.

- **Jesus:** Throughout His life, Jesus offered forgiveness and mercy to those who wronged Him, including on the cross (Luke 23:34). Imagine forgiving the very people who are executing you—talk about setting the mercy bar high! Jesus's ultimate act of mercy is a powerful reminder that we, too, can offer forgiveness and compassion, even in the most challenging circumstances.

Practical Application

Embracing and extending mercy in daily life can be quite a challenge, especially when someone cuts you off in traffic or steals your parking spot at the grocery store. But remember, even in those moments, we are called to show mercy, just as God has shown mercy to us. So next time someone wrongs you, try taking a deep breath, counting to ten, and maybe even giving them a friendly wave instead of a not-so-friendly gesture.

Learning to reflect God's mercy on us when we didn't deserve it is a humbling experience. We have all fallen short of God's glory, yet He continues to show us grace and forgiveness. As we receive this mercy, we are called to pass it along to others who may not deserve it, either. By showing mercy to those who have wronged us, we show the unconditional love of Christ and paving the way for healing and reconciliation. To bring these principles into our daily lives, try the following exercises:

1. **Simple Acts of Kindness:** Perform simple acts of kindness and mercy daily. Whether it's paying for someone's coffee, holding the door open, or simply smiling at a stranger, small gestures can make a big difference.

2. **Forgiveness Practices:** Make a habit of forgiving others and letting go of grudges. Remember, holding onto anger is like drinking poison and expecting the other person to suffer. Free yourself by embracing forgiveness.

3. **Support Charities:** Contribute to organizations that provide relief and support to those in need. Whether through financial donations, volunteering, or spreading awareness, your efforts can help extend mercy to those who need it most.

Conclusion

Learning to reflect God's own mercy on us when we didn't deserve it and passing it along to others can be easier said than done. I mean, let's be real. Sometimes it's hard to forgive someone who has hurt us deeply. But remember, God's grace is endless, and His mercy knows no bounds. So, the next time you find it hard to forgive, just think of all the times God has forgiven you for your own mistakes. It might just make extending that same forgiveness a little easier. By reflecting God's own mercy on us and passing it along to others, we can make a real difference in the world.

In a cruel world, mercy can be a powerful force for change. By embracing God's mercy and extending it to others, we can reflect His love and compassion, making the world a little less harsh and a lot more forgiving. Let's take up the challenge of being merciful, even when it's difficult. A little mercy goes a long way. Who knows? You might just make someone's day—or even their life—brighter. As we seek to live out our faith in practical ways, embracing and extending mercy should be at the forefront of our minds.

By following the examples set forth in Scripture, we can become vessels of God's mercy and love in a world that is often filled with pain and suffering. Let us strive to reflect God's mercy in all that we do, showing compassion and forgiveness to those around us as we seek to live out our faith in a meaningful and impactful way. Let's strive to be like the Good Samaritan and even Jesus Himself, showing mercy to all and spreading love and forgiveness wherever we go. Remember, a little of mercy can go a long way.

Chapter 4

Seeking Hope in an Uncertain World

Introduction: Maintaining hope in uncertain times

U NCERTAINTY IS A CONSTANT in life, much like the inevitability of finding a sock missing after laundry day. But amid the unknown, hope anchors us, giving us the strength to move forward even when the future seems as clear as a mud puddle. In times of uncertainty and difficulty, it's challenging to maintain a sense of hope and faith. The world is constantly changing, and it can feel like the ground beneath our feet is shifting. As Christians, we are called to hold fast to our hope in God, even when the future seems uncertain.

When faced with suffering and pain, it's easy to lose sight of the bigger picture. However, as followers of Christ, we know our suffering is not in vain. In Romans 8:18, we are told that our present sufferings are not worth comparing with the glory within us. This verse serves as a powerful reminder that our pain is temporary and that God has a greater plan for our lives.

In moments of doubt and wavering faith, it's easy to lose sight of the promises of God. However, we are called to trust in the Lord with all our hearts and lean not on our own understanding (Proverbs 3:5). This verse serves as a reminder that even when we cannot see the way forward, God is faithful and will guide us through the darkness. And as we navigate the complexities of mental health and wellbeing, it can be tempting to lose hope in our struggles.

However, we remember God is our refuge and strength, an ever-present help in trouble (Psalm 46:1). This verse serves as a source of comfort and encouragement, reminding us that even in our darkest moments, God is with us, offering us hope and healing.

Biblical Context: Romans 15:13: The God of hope; Hebrews 11:1: Faith and hope

In life's trials and tribulations, it's easy to lose hope. However, as Christian readers, we see in Romans 15:13 that we serve the God of hope. What does that mean? Well, it means that no matter how dark things may seem, we can trust in God to bring us hope and light. So, next time you're feeling down in the dumps, just remember that the God of hope has got your back.

This powerful verse reassures us our hope does not come from our circumstances or our own strength, but from the unchanging and unwavering hope that God provides. It's like a divine pep talk, promising that our trust in God will lead to an abundance of hope, joy, and peace. So, when we place our trust in Him, we can experience a peace and joy that transcends all understanding.

Hebrews 11:1 reminds us of the close relationship between faith and hope. It's like peanut butter and jelly, or Batman and Robin. It states, "Now faith is the assurance of things hoped for, the conviction of things not seen."

This verse challenges us to have faith in God's promises, even when we cannot see how they will come to fruition. Essentially, having faith is believing in the invisible and trusting that it's just as real as the ground beneath our feet (even if sometimes it feels like quicksand). And through faith, we can hold on to hope and trust that God is working all things together for our good. So, if you're feeling a little low on hope, just have a little faith that things will get better.

As we navigate the struggles of life, it is important to cling to the truths found in these verses. In times of doubt and uncertainty, we can turn to the words of Romans 15:13 and Hebrews 11:1 for encouragement and strength. These verses remind us that our hope is not in ourselves, but in the God Who is always faithful. May these verses serve as a beacon of light in the darkness, a source of comfort in times of struggle, and a reminder of the unshakeable hope and faith we have in our loving God. Let us trust in His promises, rely on His strength, and walk confidently in the hope He provides.

Building Hope

Ah, the age-old struggle of building hope through faith and trust in God's promises. It's like trying to assemble Ikea furniture without the instructions—you know it's possible, but it's going to take a lot of patience and maybe a few choice words. When we lean on God's promises, we can find comfort and strength even in trials and uncertainties. However, sometimes doubt sneaks in and we may struggle to trust in God's promises.

When doubt creeps in, it's like that annoying friend who always shows up uninvited and overstays their welcome. But just like you wouldn't let that friend ruin your day, don't let doubt ruin your faith in God's promises. Grab a metaphorical broom and sweep doubt right out the door! In those moments, it is important to remember that doubt is a natural part of our faith journey.

It is okay to have questions and uncertainties, but we must not let them shake our foundation of faith. Even in moments of doubt, we can trust in God's faithfulness and rely on His promises. The Bible holds many stories of doubt and uncertainty, yet God remains steadfast in his love and provision. Turn to God in prayer, seeking His guidance and understanding, and allowing Him to strengthen our trust in His promises.

1. **Trust in God's Promises:** Reflect on the assurances found in Scripture. Consider God's promises as the original "can't-break" guarantees, better than any lifetime warranty you'll ever get from a store.

2. **Stay Connected in Prayer:** Communicate regularly with God to reinforce your hope. Think of it as recharging your spiritual batteries—nobody likes a phone (or soul) at 1% power.

3. **Encourage Others:** Sharing hope with others strengthens your own. It's like a boomerang of positivity: the more you give, the more it comes back to you.

Biblical Examples

The Bible is full of characters who held onto hope despite overwhelming odds, and their stories can inspire us to do the same on our own faith journey. One powerful example of unwavering hope in the Bible comes found in the story of Abraham. Despite facing impossible circumstances, Abraham trusted in God's promise of a son and a great nation. God tested his faith time and time again, but ultimately, he remained steadfast in his belief that God would fulfill His word. This guy was told he would be the father of many nations, despite being old and childless. Talk about a leap of faith! If Abraham can trust in God's promises, surely we can, too.

Similarly, Ruth's story of loyalty and devotion to her mother-in-law, Naomi displays the power of hope and trust in God's providence. This woman's story is all about loyalty, resilience, and hope. Despite facing loss and uncertainty, Ruth trusted in God's plan for her life. And boy, did it pay off! She ended up marrying Boaz and becoming a part of Jesus' lineage. Not too shabby, Ruth!

- **Abraham:** God promised Abraham a son, which sounds straightforward until you realize he was pushing one hundred years old. Despite the biological improbabilities, Abraham trusted God's promise. And guess what? Isaac was born, proving that when God makes a promise, not even the ticking of the biological clock can stop it (Genesis 17-21). Abraham's story reminds us that hope sometimes requires patience and a sense of humor about the impossible.

- **Ruth:** Ruth's story is one of loyalty, love, and hope. After losing her husband, she stuck with her mother-in-law, Naomi, rather than return to her own family. This act of loyalty led her on a challenging journey, but her hope and faithfulness gained her a new life and family with Boaz (Book of Ruth). Ruth's story shows hope can turn dire circumstances into a beautiful new beginning.

Practical Application

To bring these principles into our daily lives, try the following exercises:

1. **Scripture Meditation:** Memorize and meditate on Bible verses about hope. It's like mental and spiritual yoga, stretching and strengthening your hope muscles.

2. **Prayer Journaling:** Document your prayers and how God answers them. This can become your personal "Book of Miracles," a tangible reminder that God listens and responds.

3. **Community Support:** Engage with a faith community for mutual encouragement. Think of it as a support group where everyone is cheering for your hope to grow and thrive.

Conclusion

When doubt creeps in and building hope seems like an impossible task, remember the Biblical examples. Trust in God's promises, even when it feels like a long shot. And as we navigate the challenges of life, let us draw inspiration from the examples of hope in the Bible and strive to emulate the unwavering faith of Abraham and Ruth. By building our hope through faith and trust in God's promises, we can find courage to face life's challenges with confidence and peace, knowing that God is always with us, guiding us towards His perfect plan for our lives. Trust in His promises, even when doubt creeps in, and watch as He works miracles in your life.

Remember that hope is vital in navigating uncertainty. By trusting in God's promises, staying connected in prayer, and encouraging others, we can always maintain a hopeful outlook. So, let's anchor ourselves in hope, knowing that no matter how unpredictable life gets, God's promises are the ultimate life raft. And who knows? You might just find that missing sock along the way.

Chapter 5

Seeking Comfort in a Mournful World

Introduction: Finding comfort in times of sorrow

G RIEF AND LOSS ARE inevitable parts of life, much like taxes and the occasional wardrobe malfunction at the worst possible moment. But amid our sorrow, God offers comfort, providing a divine shoulder to cry on. In life, we all face moments of sorrow and sadness. It is during these difficult times we may question our faith and seeking answers to the hardships we are facing. As Christians, we must turn to the Bible for guidance and comfort, trusting in the promises of God to provide us with strength and peace in times of trouble.

The Bible is a source of hope and encouragement for those who are struggling with sorrow and pain. It reminds us we are not alone in our suffering, and that God is always with us, ready to comfort and support us in our time of need. By turning to the Scriptures, we can find solace in the words of God, knowing that He is our refuge and strength in times of trouble.

As we navigate through the challenges of life, it is important to remember that while we may not always understand why we are facing trials and tribulations, we can trust in the wisdom and sovereignty of God to guide us through the darkest moments of our lives.

Finding comfort in times of sorrow requires us to have faith and trust in God's promises, and also realizing that God cares for us deeply and desires for us to live a life of abundance and joy. Through prayer, meditation, and seeking support from our Christian community, we can find solace in the arms of our loving Father, who promises to bring us peace that surpasses all understanding.

Biblical Context: Matthew 5:4: Blessed are those who mourn; 2 Corinthians 1:3-4: God of all comfort

In the Bible, even in times of mourning, blessings reach us. Matthew 5:4 comforts us with the words, "Blessed are those who mourn, for they will be comforted." This isn't just a Hallmark card sentiment; it's a profound promise from Jesus Himself. It is a powerful statement that reminds us it is okay to grieve and mourn the losses and struggles we face in life.

As Christians, we can take solace because our mourning is not in vain. God sees our pain and promises to bring us comfort in our time of need. So, if you cry over spilled milk (or something a bit more serious), take heart! God sees your tears and promises to bring you comfort in your sorrow. And hey, who doesn't love a good cry now and then? It's like a free therapy session straight from the heavens!

2 Corinthians 1:3-4 praises God as "the Father of compassion and the God of all comfort, who comforts us in all our troubles." Imagine God as the ultimate comfort blanket—always warm, always there, and never needing a wash. God is the "God of all comfort" Who comforts us in all our troubles so that we can comfort those in any trouble with the comfort we ourselves receive from God. This beautiful passage encourages us to turn to God in our times of distress, knowing that He is always there to provide us with the comfort and strength we need to persevere through our trials.

God is like the friend who always knows just what to say (or in this case, what to do). So, next time you're feeling down in the dumps, remember that you have a direct line to the God of all comfort. No need to wallow in self-pity when you've got the Big Guy on your side, ready to wrap you up in a warm blanket of love and understanding.

As we navigate the challenges of life, it's easy to lose sight of God's comforting presence in our lives. However, by meditating on these verses and seeking God's comfort in times of mourning, we can find peace and solace in our pain. Remember, God is always with us, ready to wrap us in His loving arms and provide us with the comfort and strength we need to face whatever comes our way.

God is the ultimate source of comfort and healing, so we must trust in His unfailing love and seek solace in His presence, knowing that He will never leave us or forsake us.

May we find peace in our mourning, knowing that God is with us, comforting us and guiding us through every trial and tribulation.

Let us take heart knowing God is the God of all comfort, ready and willing to provide us with the strength and solace we need to face life's toughest challenges. As we trust in Him and seek His comfort in times of mourning, may we be filled with hope and peace, knowing that He is always by our side, guiding us through every trial and tribulation. May these words serve as a reminder that we are never alone in our suffering, for God is with us, comforting us and bringing us peace in our time of need.

Finding Comfort

In times of trouble and pain, turning to God first and then to others for comfort can bring peace and solace beyond measure. As Christians, we are called to seek God's comfort in all situations, knowing that He is always there to provide us with the strength we need to endure. Not only can we seek comfort from God, but we are also called to be a source of comfort to others in their times of need. By showing compassion and empathy towards those who are suffering, we can reflect God's love and grace to those around us.

Surrendering to God's healing power in times of pain is a powerful act of faith and trust. When we acknowledge our pain and surrender it to God, we open ourselves up to His healing touch. God's healing power is limitless and can bring about miraculous transformations in our lives. By surrendering to God's healing power, we can find relief from our suffering and experience His peace that surpasses all understanding.

1. **Lean on God:** Turn to God in times of sorrow and let Him comfort you. Think of it as the ultimate divine hug, always available and never awkward.

2. **Seek Support:** Allow others to provide comfort and companionship. Even Jesus surrounded Himself with friends, and if He can do it, so can we.

3. **Express Your Grief:** A healthy expression of grief is essential for healing. Whether it's through tears, creative outlets, or even a good, old-fashioned scream into a pillow, let it out.

Biblical Examples

The stories of comfort in the Bible are not just ancient tales of long-dead heroes—they are living examples of God's love and grace in action. In fact, the contains many stories of comfort and healing and stories of individuals who found comfort in God during their darkest times. These stories provide us with inspiration and hope in our own times of need. The story of Job teaches us about perseverance in the face of suffering, as Job remained faithful to God even in his trials. He might've lost everything, but he never lost his faith in God.

Similarly, the story of David shows us the power of God's comfort and healing, as David found solace in God's presence during his darkest moments. He faced countless trials and tribulations, but always turned to God for comfort and strength. These stories remind us that God is always with us, offering comfort and healing in times of pain. Their experiences teach us about the importance of faith, perseverance, and trust in God's comfort and healing power. By studying these stories and applying their lessons to our own lives, we can find strength and hope in our struggles.

- **Job:** Job's story is the ultimate tale of "when it rains, it pours." Despite losing his health, wealth, and family, Job found solace in God. Through his immense suffering, he never wavered in his faith, ultimately experiencing God's comfort and restoration (Book of Job). Job teaches us that even when life feels like one giant catastrophe, God's comfort is ever-present.

- **David:** King David was no stranger to grief and loss. His psalms often reflect his anguish and longing for God's comfort. Psalm 23 is a perfect example: "Even though I walk through the darkest valley, I will fear no evil, for You are with me; Your rod and Your staff, they comfort me." David's raw, honest expressions of sorrow and reliance on God show us it's okay to be vulnerable and to seek divine comfort.

Practical Application

Let's be real for a moment. Mourning isn't exactly a walk in the park. It can be messy, emotional, and downright exhausting. So, when you find yourself in the depths of despair, don't be afraid to reach out for help. Whether it's through prayer, talking to a friend, or seeking professional guidance, there's no shame in asking for a little extra support during tough times. After all, even Jesus wept (John 11:35). If it's good enough for the Son of God, it's good enough for us!

The great news is that God promises to be with you in your mourning and to bring you comfort in your time of need. So, wipe away those tears, hold your head high, and remember that even in sorrow, you are blessed. And hey, a good cry never hurt anyone (except maybe your mascara). To bring these principles into our daily lives, try the following exercises:

1. **Prayer and Worship:** Spend time in prayer and worship, focusing on God's comforting presence. Think of it as a spiritual spa day, refreshing your soul and soothing your heart.

2. **Support Groups:** Join groups that provide a space for sharing grief and finding solace. Remember, sharing your load makes it lighter, and who knows? You might make good friends along the way.

3. **Counseling:** Seek professional counseling if needed to process grief. There's no shame in getting help, and a good counselor can be like a GPS, guiding you through the rough terrain of sorrow.

Conclusion

In times of trouble, we often seek solace in the arms of our loved ones or a pint of ice cream. But as Christians, we know that genuine comfort is only found in seeking God's comforting presence. God is always there to comfort you, to heal you, and to guide you through the storms. You must just trust in His love, lean on His grace, and know that you are never alone. Whether it's through prayer, meditation, or simply sitting in silence, we can find peace knowing that God is there to hold us in our times of need. But it's not just about receiving comfort from God—it's also about being a comfort to others.

As Christians, we are called to be a light in the darkness, a beacon of hope to those who are struggling. By reaching out to those in need, offering a listening ear or a helping hand, we can be the hands and feet of Christ in a world that desperately needs his love.

Surrendering to God's healing power in times of pain can be a tough concept to grasp. We may want to hold on to our pain, our anger, our resentment, but God calls us to let go, and trust in his plan for our lives. By surrendering our pain to God, we open ourselves up to his healing power, allowing him to work in us and through us to bring about restoration and wholeness.

Seeking God's comfort and being a comfort to others, surrendering to God's healing power in times of pain, and finding inspiration in the stories of Job and David are essential practices for Christian readers seeking biblical answers to life's toughest questions. By embracing these principles and turning to God in times of need, we can find peace, healing, and hope in our struggles. May we always remember that God is our ultimate source of comfort and healing, and that He is always there to guide us through life's challenges.

In a mournful world, God's comfort is a source of strength. By leaning on God, seeking support, and expressing grief, we can find solace. Remember Matthew 5:4: "Blessed are those who mourn, for they will be comforted." So, when life gives you heartaches, don't just grit your teeth and bear it. Turn to God, let others in, and allow yourself to grieve. You'll find that comfort is not only possible but promised. And who knows? You might even find a bit of unexpected joy along the way.

Chapter 6

Seeking Joy in a Gloomy World

Introduction: Discovering joy despite gloom

WITH ALL THE NEGATIVITY surrounding us through the daily news and social media, it can be challenging to find moments of joy. But take heart! It is possible to cultivate a joy rooted in God that transcends circumstances and outshines the darkest clouds. So, even though the world might be filled with darkness and despair, and we are often faced with tough questions that challenge our faith and leave us feeling lost and alone, we must remember the light that shines within us—the light of God's love and grace.

As we navigate through the trials and tribulations of life, it is important to remember that joy can still be found amidst the gloom. It is in these moments of darkness that our faith is tested and strengthened, and it is through our faith that we can find joy and hope in even the darkest of times. Joy is a gift from God that is available to us in every season of life.

By cultivating gratitude and worship, finding pleasure in God regardless of our circumstances, and learning from biblical examples of joy, we can experience a deep and lasting sense of joy that surpasses all understanding. May the examples of those who have gone before us inspire us and fill us with joy, regardless of the challenges we may face.

Biblical Context: Nehemiah 8:10: The joy of the Lord is your strength; Philippians 4:4: Rejoicing in the Lord

Are you feeling down and out? Are life's challenges weighing you down? Well, fear not, dear, for I bring you some biblical wisdom that is sure to lift your spirits and put a smile on your face. Nehemiah 8:10 encourages us, "The joy of the Lord is your strength." When we find joy in the Lord, we gain the strength to face any obstacle that comes our way. So, next time you're feeling weak or defeated, just remember to tap into the joy that comes from the Lord. This isn't just a nice thought; it's a powerful truth that joy from God can fortify us against life's hardships.

This powerful verse serves as a reminder that our strength does not come from our own power or abilities, but from the joy that comes from knowing and trusting in the Lord. When we find joy in Him, we find the strength to face whatever comes our way with confidence and resilience. So, next time you're feeling weak or overwhelmed, just remember to put on your joyful pants and tap into that divine strength!

To put a pep in your step, here's a little reminder from Philippians 4:4, where it commands, "Rejoice in the Lord always. I will say it again: Rejoice!" No matter what life throws at you, it's important to find joy in the Lord and rejoice in all circumstances. So, whether you're dealing with a tough boss, a broken relationship, or just a bad hair day, remember to take a moment to rejoice in the goodness of the Lord.

By the way, Paul's repetition here isn't because he likes the sound of his own voice—it's emphasizing the importance of constant rejoicing. This command may seem difficult to follow, especially in suffering and pain. However, when we choose to rejoice in the Lord, we are choosing to focus on His goodness, faithfulness, and promises rather than on our present circumstances. This shift in perspective can bring about a sense of peace and contentment that surpasses all understanding.

Now, I know what you're thinking, "But how can I possibly find joy in this chaos and craziness?" By trusting in the Lord and His promises, we can find joy even in the toughest of times. The joy of the Lord is your strength, and by rejoicing in Him, you can find peace and happiness in any situation. So, next time you're feeling overwhelmed, just take a deep breath, say a little prayer, and remind yourself that the joy of the Lord is your strength. So, rejoice in the Lord always. Yes, always. Even when you spill your coffee, miss your bus, or accidentally hit "reply all" on a sensitive email. Remember, the joy of the Lord is not dependent on our circumstances, but on our relationship with Him. So, rejoice, even if you're stuck in traffic or waiting in line at the DMV. It's all part of the joyous journey of life!

Our joy and strength come from the Lord. Joy is not just a fleeting emotion, but a deep-rooted sense of contentment and peace that comes from knowing and trusting in God. In times of suffering and pain, we can find comfort in His presence and the knowledge that He is working all things together for our good. By rejoicing in the Lord and finding our strength in Him, we can navigate life's challenges with grace and confidence, knowing that we are never alone. So, when life throws you a curveball or a lemon (or a curveball made of lemons), remember to lean on the joy of the Lord for your strength.

Cultivating Joy

Joy is not dependent on our external circumstances, but comes from a deep sense of gratitude and worship towards God. So, naturally, the best way to cultivate joy in our lives is through the practice of gratitude. By focusing on the blessings in our lives and expressing thankfulness to God, we can shift our perspective from what we lack to what we have been given. This attitude of gratitude can lead to a sense of joy that transcends any temporary struggles or challenges we may face. Through worship, we can also find joy in God's presence and in His promises, knowing that He is always with us, regardless of our circumstances.

Finding pleasure in God, regardless of life's circumstances, is a powerful way to experience genuine joy. When we anchor our happiness in God's unwavering love and faithfulness, we can find peace and contentment, even in trials and tribulations. By trusting in God's plan for our lives and seeking His presence daily, we can experience a deep and lasting joy that transcends our earthly circumstances.

1. **Focus on God:** Rejoice in Who God is and His blessings. This means seeing God not as a stern taskmaster, but as a loving Father Who's already given you more blessings than the number of funny cat videos on the internet.

2. **Practice Gratitude:** Regularly thank God for His goodness. If you can't think of anything, start small: "Thank you, God, for coffee. Without it, I might not have survived this morning."

3. **Engage in Worship:** Joyfully worship God in all circumstances. Think of it as the ultimate stress-reliever, better than yoga or that second slice of chocolate

cake.

Biblical Examples

Even in the toughest of circumstances, we can find pleasure in God. The Bible offers some prime examples of joy shining through, even in the bleakest situations. Several of these characters found joy while facing their biggest adversity, such as Paul and Silas when they were imprisoned for their faith, or Mary when she was told she would give birth to the Son of God, despite the difficult timing.

Despite their difficult circumstances, they worshiped God and praise Him, leading to a miraculous display of God's power and a sense of joy that could not be shaken. Despite being chained up, facing persecution, or having your life plans ruined, they sang chose to sing praises to God. And what happened? God miraculously freed them from their chains and used them to change the world!

So, next time you find yourself in a tough spot, remember that joy is not dependent on our circumstances—it comes from our relationship with God. Their stories serve as a reminder to us that joy is not dependent on our external circumstances, but on our relationship with God and our willingness to trust in His goodness.

- **Paul and Silas:** These two were the original jailhouse rockers. After being beaten and thrown into prison, they didn't sulk or plot revenge. Instead, they sang hymns of joy (Acts 16:25). Their joyful worship not only lifted their spirits but led to a miraculous prison break. Now that's what I call finding joy in unexpected places!

- **Mary:** When the angel Gabriel informed Mary of her divine pregnancy, she didn't respond with dread or anxiety (though that would've been understandable). Instead, she broke into a song of joy, celebrating God's plan for her life (Luke 1:46-55). Mary's example shows that even life-altering news can be met with joy when we trust in God's plan.

Practical Application

Are you tired of feeling down and discouraged in your faith journey? As Christians, it is essential to find pleasure in God regardless of life's circumstances. By focusing on the goodness of God and expressing gratitude for His blessings, we can experience genuine joy in our hearts. One way to cultivate joy is through the practice of gratitude. Take a moment each day to thank God for the blessings in your life, both big and small. Whether it's a sunny day, a delicious meal, or a kind word from a friend, there is always something to be thankful for.

By shifting our focus from what we lack to what we have, we can find joy in even the most challenging situations. Another key to finding joy is through worship. When we lift our voices in praise to God, we are reminded of His greatness and goodness. Singing hymns, reading Scripture, and spending time in prayer can all help us connect with God on a deeper level and experience the joy that comes from knowing Him. So, don't be shy about belting out your favorite worship songs—God loves to hear your voice! To bring these principles into our daily lives, try the following exercises:

1. **Gratitude Journal:** Keep a journal of things for which you are thankful. Start with the basics—hot showers, Wi-Fi, and comfortable shoes—and watch your list grow. Name one thing a day and review the list at the end of the year.

2. **Worship Music:** Listen to and sing worship songs that uplift your spirit. Make it a habit to have a mini concert in your car or shower. Bonus points if you do it loud enough to make the neighbors wonder what's got you so joyful.

3. **Celebrate God's Goodness:** Regularly celebrate and reflect on God's blessings. This can be through a quiet moment of reflection, sharing testimonies with friends, or even hosting a "God is Good" party with cake and all for something good that happened recently.

Conclusion

In a world filled with chaos, uncertainty, and bad reality TV shows, it's easy to lose sight of the joy that comes from knowing and serving the Lord. But as followers of Christ, we are called to be a beacon of hope and joy to those around us. So, let's embrace the joy of the Lord and spread it like rice at a Mexican wedding. And let us hold fast to the joy of the Lord as our strength and rejoice always in His presence.

And remember, when life gets tough and the storms of life threaten to overwhelm us, we can find comfort and strength in the joy that comes from knowing that we serve a God Who is greater than any challenge we may face. So, go forth with joy, dear readers, knowing that the joy of the Lord is truly our strength.

As Christians, we have the power to choose joy through gratitude, worship, and finding pleasure in God. So, let's follow the examples of Paul and Silas, and also that of Mary, and sing praises to God, no matter what life throws our way. With a joyful heart and a grateful spirit, we can find faith and hope in even the toughest of times. So, cultivate joy in your life—God is waiting to fill you with His love and peace!

Joy can be found even in a gloomy world through a focus on God, gratitude, and worship. Remember Nehemiah 8:10: "The joy of the Lord is your strength." And when life feels like a never-ending rainstorm, tap into the joy that God offers. It's a joy that defies circumstances, uplifts the spirit, and brings a smile to your face, even on the rainiest days.

Keep on cultivating gratitude, finding pleasure in God, and looking to biblical examples of joy for inspiration. And who knows, maybe you'll sing praises in your own metaphorical prison—just don't blame us if your cellmates give you weird looks. Don't be surprised if your joy becomes contagious light and laughter to those around you.

Chapter 7

Seeking Fulfillment in a Frustrating World

Introduction: Achieving fulfillment amidst frustration

I N A WORLD WHERE frustration can be as common as a poorly timed red light, pursuing fulfillment often feels like chasing after a mirage. In life, we often face challenges and obstacles that can leave us feeling frustrated and lost. Yet, even in this rollercoaster of life, true fulfillment is possible. And thankfully, we have the ultimate guidebook to navigate through these tough times—the Bible. And finding genuine fulfillment through God's purpose ensures that our lives aren't just full of busyness but brimming with meaning.

As we covered in a previous chapter, God has a plan and purpose for each one of us. Part of this plan is for us to have fulfillment in life. So, even in frustration and disappointment, we can find fulfillment by aligning with God's purpose for us. The Bible assures us we can find true fulfillment in serving Him and others. May we delight in the Lord and find our joy and satisfaction in Him alone, by serving him and serving others.

May we hold fast to the promise of abundant life that Jesus offers, knowing that He has a plan for our lives that is greater than we can imagine. And let us embrace the abundant life that Jesus offers, knowing that He is our source of true fulfillment and joy. As we journey through the challenges of life, may we always remember that God's plans for us are good, and His love for us is unending.

Biblical Context: Psalm 37:4: Delighting in the Lord; John 10:10: Abundant life

The verse in Psalm 37:4 emphasizes the importance of delighting in the Lord. The verse advises, "Take delight in the Lord, and he will give you the desires of your heart." This doesn't mean that God is a celestial vending machine dispensing wishes. Rather, when we delight in God, our desires align with His purpose, and we find true fulfillment. This verse encourages us to take joy in our relationship with God, and to find our ultimate satisfaction in Him.

When we make God the center of our lives, we will find fulfillment and purpose beyond what this world can offer. Delighting in the Lord means seeking His presence, His will, and His ways above all else. It is a reminder that true happiness comes from a deep and intimate relationship with our Creator.

John 10:10 states, "I have come that they may have life, and have it to the full." Jesus promises a life that's not just about surviving but thriving, with purpose and joy. This verse also further emphasizes the abundant life that is available to us through Christ. Jesus came so that we may have life and have it abundantly. This abundant life is not just about material blessings or worldly success, but about experiencing the fullness of God's love, grace, and mercy. It is a life filled with purpose, hope, and joy that transcends any circumstances or challenges we may face. As Christians, we are called to live in the fullness of this abundant life, to walk in faith and trust that God's plans for us are good and fulfilling.

When we combine the teachings of Psalm 37:4 and John 10:10, we see a powerful message of hope and promise. By delighting in the Lord and seeking His will above all else, we open ourselves up to experiencing the abundant life that Jesus offers. This means trusting in God's provision, surrendering our desires to His perfect plan, and finding true satisfaction in Him alone. Living in this way assures us that God will lead us towards a path of purpose and fulfillment, even in the face of trials or tribulations.

Finding Fulfillment

As Christian readers seeking fulfillment in life, it is essential to understand that true joy and satisfaction come from serving and glorifying God. When we align our lives with

His will and purpose, we experience a deep sense of fulfillment that cannot be found elsewhere. By putting God at the center of our lives and seeking to serve Him in all that we do, we open ourselves up to a level of joy and contentment that surpasses all understanding.

1. **Delight in God:** Make God your primary source of joy and satisfaction. Imagine finding joy not just in the fleeting highs of Netflix binges or social media likes, but in a deeper, more abiding presence.

2. **Pursue God's Purpose:** Align your life with God's plans and calling. This means discovering what God has uniquely wired you to do and pursuing it with gusto.

3. **Serve Others:** Fulfillment often comes through serving and blessing others. It turns out, the secret to a fulfilled life might be less about us and more about helping those around us.

Biblical Examples

Throughout the Bible, we find stories of individuals who found true fulfillment in serving and glorifying God and in aligning with God's purpose. One such example is King Solomon, who, despite his great wealth and wisdom, ultimately found that true satisfaction could only be found in following God's commands.

Similarly, Lydia, a woman mentioned in the book of Acts, experienced fulfillment in her life by opening her heart to God and allowing Him to work through her. As we reflect on these stories and seek to apply their principles to our own lives, we can find inspiration and encouragement in knowing that true fulfillment comes from serving and glorifying God. By following their examples and seeking to align our lives with God's will, we can experience a level of joy and contentment that is truly life changing. Let us strive to live our lives in a way that brings glory and honor to God, knowing that in doing so, we will find the fulfillment in our hearts long for.

- **Solomon:** Solomon was the original rich kid on the block. Despite having wealth, power, and wisdom, he realized that true fulfillment wasn't in the bling, but in God's wisdom. When God offered Solomon anything he desired, Solomon chose wisdom to lead his people (1 Kings 3:3-14). His story teaches us that fulfillment is found in seeking God's guidance over worldly gains.

- **Lydia:** Lydia was a successful businessperson selling purple cloth, which was basically the ancient equivalent of being in the high-end fashion industry. But her real fulfillment came through her faith and hospitality. When she heard Paul's message, she opened her heart and home, becoming a key supporter of the early church (Acts 16:14-15). Lydia's life shows that fulfillment comes from integrating faith into our daily lives and using our resources to bless others.

Practical Application

To apply these principles in our lives, try the following exercises:

1. **Spiritual Disciplines:** Engage in regular prayer, Bible study, and worship. Think of these as spiritual workouts that keep your faith muscles strong.

2. **Service Opportunities:** Serve others in your community. Volunteering can be like a double-shot of espresso for your soul—energizing and deeply satisfying.

3. **Reflect on God's Plan:** Regularly seek God's guidance for your life's purpose. Listen in prayer, journal your thoughts, and be open to where God is leading you.

Conclusion

Delighting in God and aligning with His purpose lead to true fulfillment. By focusing on God, pursuing His plans, and serving others, we discover a life that's not just about checking boxes but about deep, lasting satisfaction. Remember Psalm 37:4: "Take delight in the Lord, and he will give you the desires of your heart." So, when the world feels frustrating, remember that God's purpose offers a fulfillment that's rich, rewarding, and far better than anything else on our wish lists.

When we choose to embrace God's will for our lives, we open ourselves up to a level of satisfaction and fulfillment that is truly unparalleled. By surrendering our desires and plans to Him, we allow His perfect will to be done in and through us. As we walk in obedience to God, we experience a sense of peace and contentment that can only come from knowing that we are fulfilling the purpose for which we were created.

Chapter 8

Seeking Compassion in an Indifferent World

Introduction: Showing compassion in a world that rarely cares

I N A WORLD THAT often seems indifferent, cold, and uncaring—where people are more likely to swipe left on compassion than to embrace it—showing genuine care can be challenging. Yet, as followers of Christ, we are called to be a beacon of compassion in this sea of apathy and to show compassion and love for those around us. And the best way to cultivate and express compassion is drawing from Christ's perfect example.

The Bible teaches us to love our neighbors as ourselves and to treat others as we would like to be treated. Showing compassion is not always easy, but it is a fundamental aspect of living out our faith tangibly. When we encounter suffering and pain, whether in our own lives or in the lives of others, showing compassion can be a powerful way to bring comfort and healing.

By extending a hand of kindness and understanding, we can help to bear one another's burdens and share in each other's joys. And when we focus on serving others and putting their needs above our own, we can discover a deeper sense of fulfillment and purpose. By showing compassion to those around us, we can live out God's calling for our lives and make a positive impact on the world.

Showing compassion can also be a powerful way to strengthen our faith and trust in God. By reaching out to those in need and showing them the love of Christ, we can experience a renewed sense of connection to our beliefs and find comfort in knowing that we are not alone in our struggles. Showing compassion in a world that often doesn't care is a powerful way to live out our faith and make a difference in the lives of others. So, may the example of Jesus Christ, Who showed compassion to all He encountered may inspire us, and strive to follow in His footsteps as we navigate the challenges of life.

Biblical Context: Colossians 3:12: Clothing yourselves with compassion; 1 Peter 3:8: Being compassionate and humble

Colossians 3:12 instructs, "Therefore, as God's chosen people, holy and dearly loved, clothe yourselves with compassion, kindness, humility, gentleness, and patience." This verse reminds us to dress ourselves with compassion, similar to how we put on our favorite pair of jeans or that cozy sweater, but it doesn't propose a new fashion line, rather it suggests a way of life that radiates love and care. This verse reminds us that as Christians, we are called to embody these virtues in our daily lives. Compassion is not just a feeling, but an action that we must actively put on, like a garment.

When we show compassion to others, we are reflecting the love and mercy of Christ to the world. It is through our acts of compassion that we can truly make a difference in the lives of those around us. But let's be real, compassion is not exactly as easy to slip into as those comfy clothes. It takes effort and intentionality to truly embody compassion in our daily lives. So, next time you're getting dressed in the morning, remember to put on a heart full of compassion.

1 Peter 3:8 further calls us to "be like-minded, be sympathetic, love one another, be compassionate and humble." In the same way, this verse reminds us that compassion isn't an accessory but a fundamental part of our spiritual wardrobe. It emphasizes the importance of treating others with kindness and empathy, regardless of their circumstances.

As Christians, we are called to love one another as Christ loves us, and this love is best expressed through acts of compassion and humility. When we show compassion towards others, we are following in the footsteps of Jesus, who showed compassion to all those he encountered during his time on Earth.

Humility is not a popular trait in today's world where self-promotion and ego-boosting seem to be the norm. But it's time to shake things up a bit. Let's embrace humility like it's the latest fashion trend and show the world that compassion and humility never go out of style. Imagine a world where everyone is rocking compassion and humility like it's the hottest fashion statement.

Sounds like a pretty good place to live, right? So, let's challenge ourselves to embody these traits in our daily interactions with others. Who knows, you might just start a compassion revolution in your community.

In a world filled with suffering and pain, it is easy to become focused on our own needs and desires. However, when we choose to clothe ourselves with compassion and humility, we can reach out to those who are hurting and in need of love and support. By embodying these virtues, we can bring hope and healing to those who are struggling.

When we choose to live a life of compassion and humility, we can also reflect the light of Christ to the world. Our actions speak louder than words, and when we show compassion towards others, we show the love of God in a tangible way.

Let us strive to be known for our compassion and humility, so that others may see Christ in us and be drawn closer to Him. Let's take a cue from the Bible and make compassion and humility our daily uniform. Let's strive to be the best-dressed individuals in the room, not because of our fancy clothes, but because of the compassion and humility we wear on our sleeves.

Cultivating Compassion

Jesus showed us the ultimate act of compassion by sacrificing Himself for our sins. As Christians, we are called to follow in His footsteps and show compassion to those around us. By emulating Christ's love and kindness, we can truly make a difference in the lives of others. Understanding the importance of being empathetic to others is crucial in our Christian walk.

Empathy allows us to connect with people on a deeper level and truly understand their struggles and pain. When we show empathy towards others, we are reflecting the heart of God and spreading His love to those in need. Let us strive to be more compassionate in our interactions with others, just as Jesus was during His time on Earth.

1. **Reflect on God's Compassion:** Recognize and appreciate the compassion God shows us. It's like appreciating a sunrise—beautiful, life-giving, and reminding us that God's love is new every morning.

2. **Develop Empathy:** Seek to understand and share in others' feelings. This means putting ourselves in others' shoes, even if they're Crocs.

3. **Act in Love:** Demonstrate compassion through tangible acts of kindness. It's

not enough to feel compassion; we need to show it, even if it's as simple as a smile or a helping hand.

Biblical Examples

Throughout the Bible, we see many examples of acts of compassion in action. Jesus performed countless miracles: healing the sick, feeding the hungry, comforting the brokenhearted, and showing compassion to the marginalized. Jesus was the ultimate example of compassion, showing love and care for those around Him. By following His example, we can learn to see others through His eyes and extend compassion to those in need.

The Early Church also showed compassion by caring for the needy in their communities. They displayed empathy in practical ways. These biblical acts serve as a powerful reminder of the importance of showing compassion to those around us. Let us be inspired by these examples and seek to follow in their footsteps.

- **Jesus:** If compassion were an Olympic sport, Jesus would have all the gold medals. He showed compassion by healing the sick, feeding the hungry, and even weeping with those who mourned. Matthew 14:14 tells us, "When Jesus landed and saw a large crowd, He had compassion on them and healed their sick." Imagine healing a crowd just because you care—that's compassion at its finest.

- **The Early Church:** The early Christians didn't just talk the talk; they walked the walk. Acts 2:44-45 says, "All the believers were together and had everything in common. They sold property and possessions to give to anyone who had need." They practiced communal compassion by sharing resources, making sure no one remained behind. Picture a giant potluck where everyone shares their best dishes—that's the Early Church in action.

Practical Application

Understanding the importance of being empathetic to others is crucial for Christians. Empathy allows us to connect with others on a deeper level and truly understand their struggles. When we put ourselves in someone else's shoes, we can offer genuine support and comfort. So next time you encounter someone in need, remember to show empathy and compassion, just as Christ did. To bring these principles into our everyday lives, consider these practical steps:

1. **Acts of Kindness:** Regularly perform simple acts of kindness for others. Whether it's holding the door, paying for someone's coffee, or just offering a kind word, small acts can make a big difference. Think of it as spreading little seeds of compassion that grow into a beautiful garden.

2. **Listening Ear:** Offer a listening ear and support to those in need. Sometimes, the best way to show compassion is simply to listen. Channel your inner therapist and give people the space to share their burdens.

3. **Volunteer Work:** Engage in volunteer work that helps the marginalized and suffering. Find a cause that tugs at your heartstrings and get involved. Whether it's serving at a soup kitchen, tutoring kids, or helping at an animal shelter, your time and effort can bring hope and healing.

Conclusion

Biblical acts of compassion are abundant throughout the Bible. From Jesus' miraculous healings to the Early Church's care for the poor and marginalized, the importance of showing compassion is unmistakable. Jesus healed the blind, the paralyzed, and even raised the dead, showing us the power of compassion in action. The Early Church followed His example by caring for widows, orphans, and those in need.

By developing a heart of compassion through Christ's example and understanding the importance of empathy, we can make a real difference in the lives of those around us. May you strive to be like Jesus, showing love and compassion to all we meet, just as He did during His time on Earth.

Cultivating compassion in an indifferent world reflects God's love and brings a touch of Heaven to Earth. By reflecting on God's compassion, developing empathy, and acting in love, we can transform our communities one kind act at a time. Remember Colossians 3:12: "Clothe yourselves with compassion, kindness, humility, gentleness, and patience." In this spiritual wardrobe, compassion is always in style, and it never goes out of season. So, go ahead—be the person who changes the world, one act of compassion at a time.

It is important to remember the power of compassion and humility. These virtues not only benefit those around us, but they also have a positive impact on our own mental and emotional well-being. When we choose to live a life of compassion and humility, we can experience the peace and joy that comes from serving others and putting their needs above our own.

May we always seek to clothe ourselves with compassion, so that we may be a light in a world in need of love and kindness. And by following Christ's example and showing love to others, we can make a lasting impact on the world. Let us be inspired by the biblical acts of compassion and strive to be a light in a world filled with darkness. May we always remember to show love and kindness to those in need, just as Christ did.

Chapter 9

Seeking Wisdom in a Senseless World

Introduction: The pursuit of wisdom in a world lacking sense

ARE YOU TIRED OF making decisions that leave you scratching your head and wondering, "What was I thinking?" Well, fear not. I have some practical applications for gaining wisdom that will have you making choices like a boss in no time! We're diving into the biblical context of asking God for wisdom, because sometimes we all need a little divine guidance.

Navigating a world that often seems senseless and chaotic requires a special wisdom—divine wisdom that comes from God. In a world that often seems to lack sense and meaning, it's easy to feel lost and uncertain. It's like trying to solve a jigsaw puzzle with pieces from five different puzzles. However, as believers in Christ, we are called to seek wisdom and understanding in all areas of our lives. By seeking, finding, and applying God's wisdom in our lives, senseless journeys of life transform into purposeful adventures.

The Bible contains much wisdom and insight that can help us make sense of the world and find meaning in our experiences. The pursuit of wisdom in a world lacking sense is a noble and vital endeavor for all believers. By seeking biblical answers, we can find meaning, purpose, and direction in a world that often seems confusing, senseless, and chaotic. As we delve into the Word of God and seek His guidance in all areas of our lives, we can rest in the promise He will lead us on the path to wisdom and understanding. May you seek God's wisdom in all aspects of your life and trust in His plan for you.

As we delve into the practical applications of gaining wisdom through Scripture, prayer, and godly counsel, let us remember that true wisdom comes from God alone. By seeking His guidance and following His principles, we can navigate through life's toughest questions with confidence and assurance, knowing that we are walking in alignment with His will. Let us draw inspiration from the examples of wisdom in the Bible, learning from the lives of Solomon and Daniel, and applying their insights to our own journey of seeking biblical answers to life's complexities.

Don't be afraid to lean on God for wisdom in your life's toughest moments. After all, He's the ultimate life coach, and He's always just a prayer away. So go ahead, ask away, and watch as He guides you with grace through life's tricky twists and turns. Who knows, you might just make decisions that even surprise you.

Biblical Context: James 1:5: Asking God for wisdom; Proverbs 2:6: The Lord gives wisdom

The book of James reminds us of the importance of seeking wisdom from God. James 1:5 promises, "If any of you lacks wisdom, ask God, Who gives generously to all without finding fault, and it will be given to you." This is like God saying, "Hey, if you need directions, just ask, and I'll get you there without making you feel bad for being lost." It's like having a direct line to the ultimate life coach!

So next time you have a tough decision, don't just flip a coin, or consult your horoscope—ask God for wisdom. Who knows, He might just steer you in the right direction (and hopefully away from that questionable haircut you've been eyeing).

This verse serves as a powerful reminder that we do not have to navigate life's challenges alone. By turning to God and seeking His wisdom, we can find clarity and direction in confusion and uncertainty.

And speaking of wisdom, let's not forget Proverbs 2:6, where it says that the Lord gives wisdom by assuring, "For the Lord gives wisdom; from His mouth come knowledge and understanding." God's wisdom is better than any GPS or life hack we could find. It's like having a bottomless well of knowledge at your fingertips! Instead of Googling your problems or relying on that unreliable friend for advice, why not turn to the ultimate source of wisdom? Who knows, He might just surprise you with some profound insights (or at the very least, a good laugh).

This verse reassures us that wisdom is not something we have to strive for on our own, but something that is freely given to us by our loving Heavenly Father. As we seek to understand His ways and align our hearts with His will, He promises to guide us and provide us with the wisdom we need to navigate life's complexities.

The next time you find yourself at a crossroads or facing a tough decision, remember these wise words from James and Proverbs. Asking God for wisdom isn't just a suggestion—it's a significant change. And who knows, maybe He'll even throw in some extra grace and patience along the way (because let's be real, we all could use a little more of that).

When we face hard decisions or uncertain circumstances, we can turn to God for wisdom. By trusting in His guidance and seeking His will above our own, we can be confident that He will lead us on the path of righteousness and understanding.

By asking God for wisdom and trusting in His guidance, we can find the answers we seek and the peace that surpasses all understanding. May you trust in the Lord, seek His wisdom, and watch as He leads you on a path of light and truth.

Gaining Wisdom

In our journey of life, one of the most essential tools we can use is gaining wisdom through Scripture, prayer, and godly counsel. The Bible contains timeless truths and principles that can guide us in making wise decisions and navigating through the complexities of life. By immersing ourselves in God's Word, spending time in prayer, and seeking advice from wise and godly individuals, we can tap into a wellspring of divine wisdom that will illuminate our path and help us make choices that align with God's will.

Gaining wisdom through Scripture, prayer, and godly counsel enables us to see things from God's perspective and respond according to scriptural principles. When we view our circumstances through the lens of God's Word, we can discern the truth, identify God's will, and make decisions that honor Him. By aligning our thoughts and actions with scriptural principles, we can navigate through life with clarity, purpose, and integrity, knowing that we are walking in obedience to God's commands.

1. **Ask God for Wisdom:** The first step is simple yet profound—ask God for wisdom. It's like the ultimate "phone-a-friend" option in life's game show. In

your prayers, seek God's guidance and discernment, and trust that He will provide.

2. **Study Scripture:** The Bible is a treasure trove of wisdom. Regularly studying it is like mining for gold, except you get nuggets of divine insight instead of shiny rocks. Dive into Proverbs and other wisdom literature to fill your mind with God's knowledge.

3. **Learn from Others:** Surround yourself with wise and godly individuals. Think of them as your personal council of advisors, offering insights and perspectives that can steer you in the right direction. Just make sure they're the wise kind, not the "know-it-all" kind.

Biblical Examples

Let's not forget about the shining examples of wisdom in the Bible. The Bible is replete with examples of individuals who exemplified wisdom in their lives, such as King Solomon and Daniel. These guys were like the OG wisdom masters, making decisions that left everyone else in awe. Solomon, known for his unparalleled wisdom, sought the Lord's guidance and made decisions that reflected his reverence for God.

Daniel showed wisdom in the face of adversity, relying on his faith in God to navigate through challenging circumstances with courage and grace. So, take a page out of their playbook and start making choices that will have people saying, "Wow, that person is wise beyond their years!" These biblical examples serve as inspirations for us as we seek to cultivate wisdom in our own lives and apply it to our daily walk with God.

- **Solomon:** When Solomon could ask God for anything, he chose wisdom. God was so pleased that He gave Solomon unparalleled understanding and threw in riches and honor as a bonus (1 Kings 3:3-14). Solomon's story is a masterclass in asking for the right thing and getting more than you ever imagined.

- **Daniel:** Daniel's wisdom shone brightly in a foreign land. Despite being surrounded by senseless idol worship and political intrigue, he exhibited remarkable wisdom through his faith and obedience to God (Book of Daniel). Imagine being the smartest guy in the room and still being humble enough to give all the credit to God.

Practical Application

Here is the tried-and-true method of gaining wisdom: through Scripture, prayer, and godly counsel. It's like a triple threat of wisdom-seeking power! Just crack open that Bible, pray it up, and chat it up with some wise folks who have been around the block a few times. With practice, you'll quickly become a decision-making expert. Then, allow yourself to see things from God's perspective and responding according to scriptural principles.

It's like putting on those fancy glasses that make everything crystal clear. When you look at things through God's eyes, you'll be amazed at how much easier it is to navigate life's twists and turns. To bring these principles into our daily lives, consider the following steps:

1. **Daily Prayer:** Make asking for wisdom a regular part of your daily prayers. It's like checking in with your spiritual advisor every morning, ensuring you start the day with divine insight.

2. **Bible Study:** Engage in regular Bible study, focusing on books like Proverbs. These sessions are like wisdom workouts, building your spiritual muscles to handle life's challenges.

3. **Mentorship:** Seek mentors who embody godly wisdom. Their guidance can be invaluable, offering you a roadmap based on their experiences and understanding. It's like having a personal coach for your spiritual journey.

Conclusion

Let us strive to emulate the wisdom of Solomon and Daniel by diligently studying God's Word, engaging in fervent prayer, and seeking counsel from wise and godly individuals. By doing so, we can gain a deeper understanding of God's will, see things from His perspective, and respond according to His scriptural principles. May we be encouraged to walk in wisdom and discernment, trusting in God's guidance as we navigate through life's challenges with faith and obedience.

Seeking and applying God's wisdom helps us navigate a senseless world with grace and purpose. Remember James 1:5: "If any of you lacks wisdom, you should ask God, Who gives generously to all." In this journey through life, let God be your guide, turning the chaos into a beautifully orchestrated plan. And when in doubt, remember Solomon and Daniel—two guys who showed us that with God's wisdom, you can't go wrong, even in the most bewildering of circumstances.

Essentially, if you want to navigate life's toughest questions with grace and wisdom, just remember to turn to Scripture, prayer, and godly counsel. See things from God's perspective and respond according to scriptural principles. And don't forget to take a little inspiration from the wise folks in the Bible. Before you know it, you'll be making choices like a boss and leaving everyone else wondering how you got so darn wise.

Chapter 10

Seeking Freedom in a Restrictive World

Introduction: Experiencing freedom in the face of restrictions

H AVE YOU EVER FELT like you're living in a straitjacket, with restrictions and limitations holding you back from experiencing true freedom? In a world filled with rules, expectations, and limitations, true freedom can seem as elusive as finding a parking spot at the mall on Black Friday. But do not fear! In a restrictive world, there is still a way to break free and experience the freedom found in Christ.

True freedom can be elusive in a restrictive world. In fact, as Christian readers, we often face restrictions that can make us feel trapped or limited in our freedom. Whether it be physical, emotional, or spiritual constraints, it's challenging to navigate through these obstacles and maintain a sense of liberation. However, it is in these moments of restriction that we can truly experience freedom in a new and profound way. Through the Bible, we can experience the freedom that comes from Christ, transcending external limitations.

Faced with restrictions, we can turn to the Bible for guidance and wisdom on how to find true freedom. The pages of Scripture overflow with stories of individuals who faced seemingly insurmountable obstacles, yet found strength and liberation through their faith in God.

By seeking these biblical answers, we can learn how to overcome our own struggles and find a sense of freedom that transcends our circumstances. So, embrace the joy that comes from knowing that a God Who wants nothing more than for you to experience true freedom love and accepts you.

Biblical Context: Galatians 5:1: It is for freedom that Christ has set us free; John 8:36: Freedom through the Son

The book of Galatians in Chapter 5 Verse 1 reminds us, it is for freedom that Christ has set us free. Jesus didn't die on the cross, so we could live our lives in chains of doubt and fear. He wants us to break free from whatever is holding us back and embrace the freedom that comes from knowing Him. So, we must remember our freedom in Christ is a precious gift that we should cherish and uphold.

Through His sacrifice on the cross, Jesus has liberated us from the bondage of sin and death, allowing us to live a life of joy, peace, and purpose. We have been set free from the chains of legalism and bondage. We are no longer slaves to sin, but children of God with the freedom to live in His grace and love.

So, next time you feel overwhelmed by the pressures of society or the expectations of others, remember Galatians 5:1—it is for freedom that Christ has set us free. Embrace this freedom with joy and gratitude, knowing that God loves you unconditionally and has the power to break free from anything holding you back.

Picture this: you're at a buffet with all your favorite foods laid out before you. You have the freedom to choose what you want to eat and how much you want to indulge. This is the freedom we have in Christ—not just in terms of food, but in all aspects of our lives.

And speaking of freedom, John 8:36 further emphasizes the theme of freedom through the Son. Jesus declares, "If the Son has set you free, then you are free indeed." This powerful statement reminds us that true freedom comes from Jesus. It's like getting a golden ticket to Willy Wonka's chocolate factory, but even better, because it's the ticket to eternal life and joy. So why settle for anything less when we have the Son of God offering us the keys to freedom?

As we navigate through the challenges and trials of life, we can take comfort in knowing that the love and grace of our Savior has set us free. So, if you are you tired of feeling weighed down by the chains of life, all you need to break free from the chains of this world is a little of Jesus in your life! Embrace the freedom that comes through Him and know that there's no chain too strong for him to break.

As we delve deeper into the biblical context of these verses, they encourage us to reflect on the significance of our freedom in Christ. In a world filled with boundaries, it is easy to lose sight of the hope and freedom that comes from knowing Jesus. However, we must stand firm in our faith and trust that God's plan for us is one of liberation and redemption.

Our purpose and calling as Christian believers is our freedom in Christ. When we embrace the freedom that comes from a relationship with Jesus, we can fulfill the unique calling that God has placed on our lives. Let us hold fast to the truth of Galatians 5:1 and John 8:36, knowing that Christ set us free to live an abundant life.

Experiencing Freedom

In our journey as Christian believers, we are called to live in the freedom that comes from our relationship with Christ. This freedom is not a license to do as we please. Being a Christian doesn't mean we get a free pass to do whatever we want. Instead, it is a calling to walk in love and respect towards others while honoring societal boundaries. It is a delicate balance of living authentically in Christ while being mindful of the world. By seeking God's wisdom and guidance, we can navigate this tension with grace and humility.

Societal boundaries are there for a reason, so, while it's perfectly fine to enjoy the freedoms that come with being a Christian, it's also important to remember that there are certain boundaries that should stay in place.

Finding freedom in God's presence is a transformative experience that can bring healing and restoration to our souls. When we draw near to God through prayer, worship, and meditation on His Word, we remember of His love and faithfulness towards us. In His presence, we find the courage to let go of our fears and insecurities, trusting in His plans for our lives.

It is in the stillness of His presence that we discover true freedom and peace that surpasses all understanding. So, first, accept the freedom that comes from a relationship with Christ, then walk in the Spirit to experience this true freedom, and last, avoid returning to the things that enslave you.

1. **Freedom in God's Presence:** In God's presence, there is no need to hide or pretend to be someone you're not. He sees you exactly as you are, flaws and all, and loves you unconditionally. Let go of the chains of perfectionism and embrace the freedom that comes from being fully known and fully loved by your Creator.

2. **Breaking The Chains of Legalism:** Jesus didn't come to Earth to burden us with a laundry list of do's and don'ts. He came to set us free from the chains of legalism and offer us a life of abundant grace and freedom. Remember that grace saved you, not by your ability to follow a set of rules perfectly. Let go of the guilt and shame that often accompany legalism and instead embrace the forgiveness and love that Christ offers us freely.

3. **Freedom in Surrendering:** Surrendering doesn't mean giving up. It means letting go of the need to have everything figured out and trusting God to guide you. Let go of the need to be in control and instead open yourself up to the possibilities that come with trusting in God's plan for you. Surrendering is a way to find freedom in restriction. It may not always be easy, but it will be worth it in the end.

Biblical Examples

Let's dive into some stories of biblical freedom that will inspire and encourage you on your own journey. The stories of biblical freedom serve as powerful examples of God's faithfulness and deliverance. The Israelites' exodus from Egypt reminds us of God's power to set His people free from bondage and oppression. Talk about breaking free from societal constraints—these guys literally walked out of slavery and into the promised land, all thanks to God's faithfulness and provision. If they can do it, so can you!

And Paul's ministry illustrates the transformative power of God's grace in a person's life, turning a persecutor of Christians into a passionate follower of Christ. Despite facing persecution, imprisonment, and even shipwrecks, Paul never wavered in his commitment to spreading the gospel. He found true freedom in serving God wholeheartedly, no matter the cost. So, the next time you're feeling weighed down by the pressures of society, just remember—you have the freedom to live boldly and passionately for Christ, just like Paul did. These stories inspire us to trust in God's ability to bring freedom and redemption into our own lives, no matter how dire our circumstances may seem.

- **The Israelites:** The Israelites experienced freedom from Egyptian bondage through God's deliverance (Exodus). If you thought your Monday morning commute was rough, just wait until you hear about their journey out of Egypt. Talk about a traffic jam! Despite being enslaved for centuries in Egypt, the

Israelites wanted to break free from the chains of oppression. They had to deal with plagues, parted seas, and even a desert detour that would make Google Maps throw up its hands in defeat. But through it all, the Israelites kept faith in the ultimate freedom fighter—God Himself. They may have grumbled and complained along the way (seriously, who wouldn't after wandering in the desert for 40 years?), but they ultimately trusted in the plan that God had laid out for them.

- **Paul:** Paul lived in spiritual freedom despite physical imprisonment (Philippians 1). In Philippians 1, we see Paul writing from prison, yet his spirit is anything but defeated. Talk about making the best of a bad situation! Despite facing persecution and imprisonment, Paul remained steadfast in his faith and continued to spread the message of Christ. He didn't let his circumstances dictate his attitude or outlook—now that's some serious #FaithGoals right there! Paul reminds us that true freedom comes from our relationship with Christ. It's not about breaking free from external constraints, but about finding inner peace and contentment in chaos. So, the next time you feel you're trapped in a restrictive world, remember Paul's words and lean on the strength of Christ to set you free.

Practical Application

One key to finding freedom in God's presence is learning to let go of the things that hold us back. It's like trying to run a marathon with a giant boulder strapped to your back—sure, you might eventually make it to the finish line, but wouldn't it be so much easier if you just let go of the boulder? In God's presence, we can shed all of those burdens and truly experience the freedom that comes from surrendering to His will. Resist bondage by putting these things into practice:

1. **Spiritual Practices:** Engage in practices that reinforce your freedom in Christ, such as resisting the urge to be in control all the time and trusting God.

2. **Community Support:** Surround yourself with a supportive community of fellow believers as you work towards breaking free from the things that enslave you.

3. **Personal Reflection:** Regularly reflect on areas where you need to embrace

freedom and what chains hold you back. Is it fear, self-doubt, or maybe even an addiction to social media? Whatever it may be, it's time to identify those chains and start working towards breaking them.

Conclusion

In a world that tries to confine us to boxes labeled "acceptable" and "normal," it's easy to feel like a square peg trying to fit into a round hole. But in Christ, we are free to be our authentic, quirky, and wonderfully unique selves. Imagine a world where you can wear socks with sandals, eat ice cream for breakfast, and binge—watch Hallmark movies guilt—free. That's the freedom Christ offers us—a freedom that transcends societal norms and cultural expectations.

True freedom may be elusive in a restrictive world, but in Christ, we have the ultimate freedom that will always remain. So, break free from the chains of expectation, embrace your quirks and imperfections, and revel in the freedom that comes from knowing and following our Savior.

Remember, it's okay to wear socks with sandals—just maybe not on a first date. Of course, experiencing this freedom doesn't mean you can suddenly ignore all the rules of society. You can't just walk into a store and start taking whatever you want because "Jesus set you free." No, no, my friends, that's not how it works. The freedom that comes from Christ is freedom of the spirit, freedom to love, to forgive, to serve others, and to live in harmony with God's will.

True freedom is found in Christ alone. And this freedom found in Christ transcends external restrictions. It is freedom that empowers us to live with purpose and passion, knowing that our Heavenly Father loves and cherishes us. Let us embrace this freedom with gratitude and humility, walking in obedience to God's Word while still respecting the boundaries of society. May we find solace in God's presence and draw inspiration from the stories of biblical freedom, trusting in His faithfulness to guide us through life's challenges.

Let's not be like those stubborn Israelites wandering in the desert for forty years when they could have reached the Promised Land in a fraction of the time. Let's embrace the freedom that Christ offers us and live our lives to the fullest, knowing that we are loved and cherished by the one who set us free. Let's remember that true freedom comes from surrendering our lives to Jesus and allowing Him to guide us on the path to righteousness.

Let's throw off the chains of doubt and fear and walk boldly in the freedom that Christ has given us.

True freedom in Christ is not about doing whatever we want, but about living in obedience to His will. Living in the freedom of Christ while respecting societal boundaries is also not only possible, but it's also incredibly liberating. It's about letting go of our own desires and surrendering to His plan for our lives, knowing that His plan is always better. By finding freedom in God's presence and drawing inspiration from biblical stories of freedom, you can navigate life's toughest questions with confidence and joy.

A life of joy should mark this freedom in Christ because it means breaking free from the chains that bind us and embracing the abundant life that our Savior has promised us. So go forth with joy, knowing that you are truly free in Christ. Live in the freedom that Christ has so graciously given you—the world is waiting for your light to shine!

Chapter 11

Seeking Truth in a Deceptive World

Introduction: Finding truth amidst deception

W E OFTEN FACE THE challenge of discerning truth from deception in a world filled with conflicting messages and ideologies. It's easy to be swayed by the opinions of others or the latest trends; but as followers of Christ, it is essential that we seek the ultimate truth ... Truth, with a capital T.

Unfortunately, in a world where misinformation spreads faster than a meme and where truth seems to play hide-and-seek, finding and holding onto truth is like trying to find a needle in a haystack—but if the haystack were also on fire and spinning. But fear not! We can seek—and find—truth through God's Word and the help of the Holy Spirit, Who makes it as clear as day even when the world is murky.

In a world where deception runs rampant, it's difficult to know who or what to trust. From fake news and false prophets, the enemy seeks to lead us astray and away from the truth of God's word.

However, as Christians, we are called to be vigilant and discerning, testing everything against the standard of Scripture. By doing so, we can ensure the lies of the enemy do not lead astray us, but stand firm in the truth of God's word. Finding truth amidst deception will guide us in our journey of answering life's toughest questions.

By seeking solace in the truth of Christ, we can find peace and restoration for our minds and hearts. As Christian readers seeking answers to life's toughest questions, let us hold fast to the truth of Jesus Christ, knowing that it is the key to true freedom and fulfillment in our lives.

Biblical Context: John 14:6: Jesus is the truth; John 8:32: The truth sets you free

In the Gospel of John, two powerful verses stand out as guiding lights for Christians seeking truth and freedom. First, Jesus himself cuts through the noise with a mic-drop moment in John 14:6: "I am the way, the truth, and the life. No one comes to the Father except through Me." Talk about setting the record straight! Jesus doesn't beat around the bush—He IS the Truth. It's like He's saying, "You want the truth? Well, here I am!" Here, Jesus declares He is the Truth, emphasizing that all true knowledge and understanding come from Him.

This verse reminds us that Jesus is not just a teacher or a prophet, but the ultimate source of wisdom and knowledge. As Christian readers, we can take comfort in knowing that our faith builds on the foundation of truth found in Jesus Christ. So, if you're ever in doubt about what to believe, just remember that Jesus has got your back. And hey, if Jesus says He's the truth, who are we to argue?

Then, John 8:32 then promises this truth bomb, "You will know the truth, and the truth will set you free." Ah, freedom—who doesn't love that? Jesus isn't just talking about breaking free from physical chains here, folks. He's talking about the freedom that comes from knowing the ultimate truth. So, if you're feeling a bit trapped in life's struggles, remember that the truth is your ticket to liberation.

And hey, who doesn't want a little slice of freedom pie? Not just free from confusion, but free from the chains of deception. This verse further expands on the concept of truth by stating that the truth sets us free. This verse speaks to the transformative power of truth in our lives, breaking chains of bondage and leading us to a life of freedom and liberation. As we seek to navigate life's toughest questions, we can find solace in the promise that the truth revealed through Jesus Christ will ultimately set us free from fear, doubt, and uncertainty.

Finding Truth

First, we must, as followers of Christ, we should be diligent in our pursuit of Truth, with a capital T. Jesus Himself said, "I am the way, the truth, and the life." It all begins and ends with Jesus. Next, as Christians, we have the incredible gift of the Holy Spirit guiding us in all truth. So, when faced with difficult decisions or confusing situations, we can rely on the Holy Spirit to give us clarity and wisdom. In fact, it is crucial to rely on the guidance of the Holy Spirit and the truth found in Scripture for discernment.

The Holy Spirit is our helper and advocate, leading us into all truth and helping us discern God's will for our lives. By immersing ourselves in the Word of God, we can sharpen our discernment skills and distinguish between what is of God and what is not. Through prayer and meditation on Scripture, we can cultivate a deep sensitivity to the promptings of the Holy Spirit, enabling us to make wise decisions and navigate life's complexities with confidence.

Last, in times of doubt and uncertainty, it is essential to anchor ourselves in God's truth. We all have moments of uncertainty and insecurity. But as believers, we can combat these doubts by clinging to the promises and truths found in God's Word. We can combat personal doubts by saturating our minds with the promises and truths of God's Word.

By meditating on Scriptures that speak to our specific doubts and fears, we can find comfort, strength, and assurance in the unchanging nature of God's character. Through prayer and reflection, we can surrender our doubts to God and allow His truth to renew our minds and transform our hearts. With faith in God's promises, we can overcome doubt and walk confidently into His truth.

1. **Seek Jesus:** Start by focusing on Jesus, the embodiment of Truth. It's like tuning your radio to the only station that isn't full of static. Jesus provides clarity in a world full of contradictory signals.

2. **Study Scripture:** The Bible is the ultimate source of truth. Think of it as the original "fact-checker" before fact-checking was cool. Regular Bible study helps anchor your understanding of God's timeless truth.

3. **Discern Through the Spirit:** Rely on the Holy Spirit for discernment and understanding. The Holy Spirit is like having an internal compass that always points true north, guiding you through life's foggy moments.

Biblical Examples

The Bible gives us excellent role models in the quest for truth. We can learn valuable lessons from the Bereans' and Jesus' teachings. The Bereans were commended for their eagerness and diligence in examining and searching the Scriptures daily to verify the truth of the gospel and the teachings they were hearing.

Like the Bereans, we should approach the Bible with an open mind and a willingness to search for truth, allowing the Holy Spirit to illuminate its meaning and relevance to our lives. Jesus' teachings also provide a blueprint for seeking truth with humility, integrity, and discernment. By studying His words and following His example, we can grow in wisdom and understanding, and walk in the light of His truth.

- **The Bereans:** These folks were the original skeptics in the best way possible. They didn't just take Paul's word for it; they examined the Scriptures daily to verify the truth (Acts 17:11). Imagine them as the diligent students who double-check everything and still get straight A's.

- **Jesus:** Consistently upheld and spoke the truth in His teachings. Take the Sermon on the Mount, for example. Jesus laid down truths that were counter-cultural and revolutionary, showing that truth doesn't always align with popular opinion but with God's word.

Practical Application

To navigate the sea of deception, put these principles into practice:

1. **Bible Study:** Make regular Bible study a priority to understand God's truth. It's like doing daily mental workouts to keep your truth muscles in shape.

2. **Pray for Discernment:** Ask for the Holy Spirit's guidance in discerning truth from deception. It's like having a personal trainer who knows exactly what you need to stay spiritually fit.

3. **Truthful Living:** Commit to living truthfully in all aspects of life. This means being honest in your dealings, transparent in your actions, and authentic in your relationships. In a world of filters and facades, be the real deal.

Conclusion

As Christians, we must approach discernment, doubt, and truth with faith, humility, and reliance on God's Word. By engaging with the Holy Spirit, Scripture, and the teachings of Jesus, we can cultivate a deep understanding of God's truth and apply it to every aspect of our lives. Through prayer, meditation, and study, we can navigate life's challenges with confidence, knowing that God's truth will guide us, sustain us, and lead us into a deeper relationship with Him.

By relying on the Holy Spirit and Scripture for discernment, overcoming personal doubts about God's truth, and embracing a biblical pursuit of truth, we can confidently navigate life's toughest questions with humor and grace. Remember, God's word is a lamp unto our feet and a light unto our path. So, let's keep seeking, keep trusting, and keep laughing along the way!

In a deceptive world, we must seek and uphold God's truth with the tenacity of a treasure hunter and the joy of finding that X marks the spot. Remember John 8:32: "Then you will know the truth, and the truth will set you free." So, let's turn off the noise, tune into God's Word, and live out the truth in every aspect of our lives. Because in the end, truth ... real Truth with a capital T isn't just a concept; it's a person—Jesus—and living in His truth is the ultimate freedom. May His inspiration lead us to seek truth with courage and conviction, trusting in the unchanging wisdom and love of our Heavenly Father.

Chapter 12

Seeking Peace in a Distressful World

Introduction: Attaining peace in times of distress

I N LIFE'S CHAOS AND uncertainty, it's easy to feel overwhelmed and anxious. Thankfully, the Bible offers us some comforting words of wisdom to help us find peace in the storm. Ah, peace—a rare gem in the chaos of our world. But let's be honest, it's true; in times of distress and turmoil, it's often challenging to find peace and solace in chaos.

For as all, the goal is to attain peace that surpasses all understanding, even in the darkest of times. In this chapter, we'll delve into how to find that elusive tranquility through God, Who offers a peace that's so good, it surpasses understanding. So, buckle up, folks, because we're diving deep into the calm amidst the storm.

The Bible lets us know God is always there to comfort us and guide us, even through the darkest of times. God cares deeply for our spiritual, physical, emotional, and mental health. By turning to the Bible for comfort and seeking the support of our Christian community, we can find the strength to overcome our struggles and find peace in chaos. Through prayer and reflection, we can find the courage to seek professional help when needed and trust in God's plan for our mental health and wellbeing.

We can find peace in knowing that God is with us in our suffering and that He will never leave us nor forsake us. By surrendering our plans to Him and trusting in His timing, we can find peace in knowing that He has a purpose and a calling for each of us. By deepening our faith through prayer, study of Scripture, and fellowship with other believers, we can find peace in doubt and uncertainty, knowing that God is faithful.

And we can also gain that peace that brings healing. Mental health and wellbeing are crucial aspects of our overall well-being, yet they are unfortunately often overlooked in the Christian community. As followers of Christ, we are called to care for our minds, bodies, and spirits, recognizing that our mental health is just as important as our physical health. And by seeking Biblical wisdom and guidance, we can find peace and healing in times of distress, knowing that God is the ultimate source of our strength and comfort.

Biblical Context: Philippians 4:7: Peace of God; Isaiah 26:3: Perfect peace

In life's storms and uncertainties, many of us search for peace that surpasses all understanding. The Bible offers us guidance and reassurance in Philippians 4:7, where we are told that the peace of God, which transcends all understanding, will guard our hearts and minds in Christ Jesus.

This verse reminds us that no matter what challenges we may face, we can find solace and security in the unshakeable peace that comes from God. It's like having a fortress around your heart and mind—no worries can breach that! So, the next time you stress out over the little things, just remember that God's got you covered with his infinite peace. And let's be real. Who couldn't use a little more peace in their lives?

Now, if you're anything like me, you think, "That's great, but how do I actually tap into this peace of God?" Well, fear not, my fellow seekers of biblical answers, for Isaiah 26:3 has got your back. This verse reminds us that God will keep us in perfect peace if we keep our minds focused on Him.

This verse also further emphasizes the importance of seeking not just peace, but perfect peace in God. When we fix our minds on God and trust in Him wholeheartedly, He will keep us in perfect peace. This perfect peace is not dependent on external circumstances, but on our unwavering faith in God's sovereignty and goodness. It is a peace that can sustain us through the darkest of times and give us hope for the future. Steadfast minds and perfect peace? Sign me up! So, next time your mind wanders into the land of worry and doubt, just remember to shift your focus back to God and watch as that perfect peace washes over you like a wave of calm in a stormy sea.

Through these verses, we can take comfort because God offers us a peace that is beyond human comprehension. This peace is not fleeting or temporary, but a constant presence in our lives that provides us with strength and courage to face whatever challenges may come our way. It is a peace that fills us with hope and reminds us we are never alone in our struggles. In times of suffering and pain, it's easy to feel overwhelmed and lost.

However, the peace of God and His promise of perfect peace can serve as a beacon of light in the darkness. So, let us hold fast to the promise of Philippians 4:7 and Isaiah 26:3, trusting in God's faithfulness to provide us with the peace that we seek. May we find comfort in His presence, strength in His promises, and hope in His unfailing love. As we navigate life's challenges and uncertainties, let us remember that the peace of God is always available to us, ready to guard our hearts and minds and lead us to a place of perfect peace.

Attaining Peace

In the journey towards inner peace, one of the most powerful tools we have is our trust in God. By placing our faith in Him, we can find a sense of calm and assurance that surpasses all understanding. When we fully surrender to His will and trust in His plan for our lives, we can experience a peace that transcends our circumstances. This trust in God allows us to let go of our worries and fears, knowing that He is in control and will guide us through even the most difficult times.

Finding and living in peace during trials and difficult times is a challenge that many of us face. However, we have the assurance that God is with us every step of the way. By turning to Him in prayer and seeking His guidance, we can find the strength to persevere through even the darkest of times. It is these trials that test our faith and strengthen it, ultimately leading us to a deeper sense of peace and trust in God's plan for our lives.

1. **Trust in God:** Picture this: God, the ultimate life coach, offering His playbook for how to navigate life's twists and turns. Trusting in His sovereignty and goodness is like having the best strategy guide ever.

2. **Focus on God:** Ever tried to balance on a tightrope while juggling flaming torches? Keeping your mind steadfast on God and His promises is the ultimate balancing act. It's like finding your center amidst the circus of life.

3. **Practice Prayer and Meditation:** Forget those trendy meditation

apps—though they may help (nothing against them and you can certainly use them). Remember that God's Word is the OG meditation guide. Regular prayer and meditation on Scripture are like soul spa sessions, rejuvenating your spirit with peace you won't find in a spa package.

Biblical Examples

The Bible holds many examples of peace in chaos and turmoil. One of the most powerful examples is Jesus calming the storm, found in the book of Matthew. In this story, Jesus exhibits His power over the forces of nature, calming the raging sea with just a word. This serves as a powerful reminder that even in life's storms, we can find peace and solace in His presence.

Another example of finding peace in the Bible is through the Psalms of David. That guy knew a thing or two about finding peace in chaos. Whether he was facing giants or fleeing from enemies, David always turned to God for strength and guidance. Despite facing several trials and challenges throughout his life, David continually turned to God in prayer and found peace in His presence. His psalms are a testament to the power of faith and trust in God, even in the face of adversity. And hey, if a shepherd boy turned king can find peace through trust in God, then surely we can too, right?

- **Jesus:** Talk about cool under pressure! Jesus displayed peace during a storm that would have sent any meteorologist running for cover (Mark 4:35-41). He's the calm in the eye of every storm.

- **David:** From shepherd boy to king, David found peace in God's presence and guidance (Psalm 23). It's like he had his own personal GPS, navigating him through life's wilderness.

Practical Application

So, how can trusting in God lead to inner peace? Well, it's simple really. When we put our faith in God and trust He has a plan for us, we can let go of our worries and fears. We can rest easy knowing that He's got our backs. But wait, there's more! Not only can trusting in God bring us inner peace, but it can also help us find and live in peace even during trials and difficult times. I mean, if Jesus can stay cool as a cucumber while walking on water and calming storms, then surely we can handle a little adversity, right? So next time life gets tough, just remember to channel your inner Jesus and ride out the storm with grace and peace. To bring that biblical peace into your daily grind:

1. **Daily Devotion:** Start your day with a hearty dose of God's Word and prayer. It's like morning coffee for the soul—kick-starting your day with divine peace.

2. **Mindfulness Practices:** Engage in practices that promote peace and calm, like deep breathing and meditation. It's not just trendy; it's biblical!

3. **Positive Community:** Surround yourself with a tribe that's all about fostering peace. Like-minded folks who radiate God's peace can turn any gathering into a peace summit.

Conclusion

Finding peace in life's chaos is easier said than done. We live in a world that is constantly bombarding us with stress and anxiety, making it feel like finding peace is akin to finding a unicorn—rare and elusive. But the Bible is full of promises that remind us that God's peace is not only real, but accessible to all who seek it with a sincere heart. So, the next you feel you're about to lose your marbles, just take a deep breath and remember the words of Philippians 4:7 and Isaiah 26:3.

Remind yourself that God's peace is available to you in abundance. All you have to do is reach out and grab hold of it. And who knows, maybe you'll find that peace is not as elusive as you once thought. After all, if God can part the Red Sea and raise the dead, surely, He can bring a little peace into your life, right?

Let us remember that true peace comes from trusting in God's plan for our lives. By following the examples set forth in the Bible, we can find and live in peace even during the most difficult times. May we take comfort in the knowledge God is always with us, guiding us towards a life filled with peace, purpose, and joy.

In a world spinning with distress, God offers us a peace that's not just a band-aid—it's a suit of armor. By trusting in Him, keeping our focus on His promises, and diving deep into prayer and meditation, we can experience His perfect peace. Remember Isaiah 26:3: "You will keep in perfect peace those whose minds are steadfast, because they trust in you."

So, let's strap on that peace armor and march through life's battles, knowing that with God, peace isn't just a wish—it's a promise. So, let the peace of God wash over you like a warm blanket on a chilly night, and watch as your worries and fears melt away.

The next time you're feeling overwhelmed or anxious, just remember to trust in God and find peace in His presence. Whether you're facing a stormy sea or a giant problem, know that you are never alone. So, take a deep breath, say a brief prayer, and trust that God's got this. After all, if He can handle parting the Red Sea, then I'm pretty sure He can manage whatever life throws your way. Peace out!

Chapter 13

Seeking Rest in a Chaotic World

Introduction: Finding rest amidst chaos

ARE YOU FEELING EXHAUSTED and overwhelmed by life's demands? In this chapter, we're diving into the search for that elusive, yet oh-so-necessary thing called rest. Get ready to discover how to kick back, relax, and find true rest in life's chaos. Picture this: you're on a roller coaster called Life, and it feels like the loops and twists never end. In chaos and turmoil, finding rest can seem like an impossible task. Is it even possible to experience true rest in life's constant storms?

Thankfully, the Bible offers us a source of peace and solace, reminding us that even in the darkest moments, God is always there to provide us with rest for our weary souls. And we can find solace and peace in the knowledge God is always by our side, offering us a place of refuge and rest in chaos.

As we navigate the trials and tribulations of life, it is easy to become overwhelmed by the chaos that surrounds us. However, the Scriptures remind us that God is our ultimate source of rest and peace. In Matthew 11:28, Jesus says, "Come to me, all you who are weary and burdened, and I will give you rest."

This promise serves as a beacon of hope for Christian readers, reminding us we can always find rest in the loving arms of our Savior, no matter how chaotic our lives may seem. So, let us remember that true rest can only be found in God. May we find solace in

His promises, comfort in His presence, and peace in His love. Let us trust in the Lord to provide us with the rest we so desperately seek, even in chaos and turmoil.

Biblical Context: Matthew 11:28: Jesus' invitation to rest; Psalm 23:2: Rest in green pastures

In life's chaos and struggles, in Matthew 11:28, Jesus invites all who are weary and burdened: "Come to Me, all you who are weary and burdened, and I will give you rest." How comforting is that? It's like Jesus is the ultimate stress-relief guru, offering us a divine massage for our tired souls. So, next time you feel you're carrying the weight of the world on your shoulders, remember that Jesus is there to help you lighten the load. Seriously, this powerful verse serves as a reminder that we do not have to carry our burdens alone.

Jesus is there, waiting for us to come to Him and find rest for our souls. And in a world filled with stress and anxiety, this invitation to rest in Jesus is a beacon of hope for all who are seeking peace and comfort. It's like Jesus is handing out free passes to the ultimate chill-out zone. Why wouldn't we accept this invitation?

Then, Psalm 23:2 paints a beautiful, serene picture: "He makes me lie down in green pastures; He leads me beside quiet waters." Ah, green pastures, and quiet waters—sounds like the perfect vacation spot, doesn't it? It's like God is the ultimate travel agent, arranging the most peaceful and rejuvenating getaways for our weary hearts. It's the perfect spa day, divine style.

This verse is a beautiful picture of rest in green pastures, reminding us of the abundance and provision that God offers to His children. Just as a shepherd leads his sheep to lush green fields where they can graze and rest, so too does our Heavenly Father provide us with everything we need to find solace and rejuvenation in Him. In times of exhaustion and weariness, we can find refuge in God's presence, knowing that He sustains us and refreshes our spirits.

So, the next time life gets too hectic, just imagine yourself lounging in those green pastures, sipping on some metaphorical lemonade, and soaking up the serenity.

We can take comfort in the promise of rest that Jesus offers us. In a world that constantly demands our attention and energy, it is easy to become overwhelmed and burned out. But through prayer, meditation on God's Word, and seeking His presence, we can find the rest and renewal that our souls crave.

So, we must always remember whenever we feel burdened by the weight of our struggles, we can turn to Jesus and lay our burdens at His feet. He is always ready and willing to bear our burdens for us, offering us a yoke that is easy and a burden that is light. By surrendering our worries and fears to Him, we can experience true rest and peace that surpasses all understanding.

Let us heed the invitation of Jesus in Matthew 11:28 and find rest in Him. Let us trust in the provision and care of our Heavenly Father, knowing that He will lead us to green pastures where we can find solace and strength. In times of suffering, doubt, and uncertainty, may we turn to God for the rest and renewal that our souls desperately need?

Rest is not a sign of weakness, but a necessary part of living a balanced and fulfilling life. So, take a step back, embrace Sabbath rest and spiritual practices, nurture your mental health through meditation, and find inspiration in the biblical examples of rest. And who knows, you might just find that a little of rest can go a long way in helping you navigate life's toughest questions with faith and grace.

Finding Rest

In our fast-paced and hectic world, it's easy to overlook the importance of rest and spiritual practices. However, as Christians, it is crucial that we prioritize Sabbath rest and incorporate spiritual practices into our daily lives. Embracing Sabbath rest allows us to pause, reflect, and connect with God on a deeper level. By setting aside time for rest and spiritual practices, we can rejuvenate our souls and find peace in chaos.

Nurturing your mental health is essential for overall wellbeing, and systematic rest and meditation play a crucial role in achieving this. Resting and recharging not only benefits our physical health but also has a positive impact on our mental and emotional well-being. By incorporating meditation into our daily routine, we can quiet our minds, reduce stress, and cultivate a sense of inner peace. Through systematic rest and meditation, we can better align ourselves with God's will and find clarity in our thoughts and actions.

1. **Accept Jesus' Invitation:** Imagine Jesus as your personal relaxation guru, offering you a massage for your soul. Turning to Him brings not just relief but renewal.

2. **Practice Sabbath:** Ever tried a spiritual spa day? Embrace regular times of rest and reflection—Sabbath isn't just a day off; it's a divine reset button.

3. **Trust in God's Care:** Let God be your concierge. His provision and protection are like having a VIP pass on life's challenges.

Biblical Examples

Throughout the Bible, we see examples of the importance of rest and renewal. In Genesis, we read about God resting on the seventh day after creating the world, setting an example for us to follow. Elijah, a powerful prophet, experienced a period of burnout and exhaustion, but through God's grace, he could find renewal and strength.

From God's creation rest on the seventh day to Elijah's renewal after facing his fears, the Bible is full of stories that remind us of the importance of taking time to rest and recharge.

So go ahead, let these examples serve as a reminder that even the strongest among us need moments of rest and renewal. These biblical examples remind us of the importance of rest in our lives and the power of God's presence in times of weariness and struggle.

- **God's Creation Rest:** Even God took a breather after creating the universe (Genesis 2:2-3). If the Creator of everything can rest, so can we!

- **Elijah:** Talk about needing a vacation—Elijah found rest and renewal through God's care after a major showdown (1 Kings 19:3-9). He's proof that even the mightiest warriors need downtime. At some point, Elijah was so mad he wanted to die. God responded by providing food for him and having him take a nap. Elijah ate, slept, and realized that things weren't that bad. So, never underestimate the spiritual power of a snack and a nap.

Practical Application

Taking time out of your busy schedule to rest and connect with God is essential for maintaining a healthy and balanced life. So go ahead, put down that never-ending to-do list and take a moment to breathe in God's peace. Trust me, your soul will thank you. Nurturing your mental health through systematic rest and meditation is fundamental in life.

It's no secret that our minds can become cluttered and overwhelmed by the stresses of daily life. But by taking intentional steps to rest and meditate on God's Word, you can find peace and clarity in chaos. So go ahead, find a quiet spot, close your eyes, and let God's presence wash over you like a wave of tranquility. To bring that biblical rest into your everyday hustle:

1. **Sabbath Observance:** Set aside regular times to unplug and unwind. It's not just good for your soul; it's a biblical mandate (and even one of the Ten Commandments)!

2. **Daily Rest Practices:** Incorporate moments of peace throughout your day—quiet time, prayer breaks, or even just a deep breath amidst the chaos.

3. **Simplify Life:** Cut out unnecessary busyness. It's about focusing on what truly brings peace and joy—not just checking off boxes.

Conclusion

It is important to remember the significance of Sabbath rest and spiritual practices in our journey of faith. By prioritizing rest and incorporating spiritual practices into our daily lives, we can deepen our relationship with God and find peace in life's challenges. Just as God rested after creating the world and renewed Elijah in his time of need, we, too, can find rest and renewal in God's presence.

So, let us take inspiration from these biblical examples of rest and renewal, and consciously prioritize Sabbath rest and spiritual practices in our lives. Through systematic rest, meditation, and connection with God, we can nurture our mental health, find strength in times of weariness, and experience the peace that surpasses all understanding. May we embrace Sabbath rest and spiritual practices with open hearts and minds, trusting in God's guidance and provision every step of the way.

In a world spinning at breakneck speed, God offers us a refuge of rest. By accepting Jesus' invitation, practicing the Sabbath, and trusting in God's care, we can find the rest that rejuvenates our souls, even in the chaos. Remember Matthew 11:28: "Come to Me, all you who are weary and burdened, and I will give you rest." So, take a deep breath, lean into God's promise of rest, and let Him be your guide to finding peace amidst life's roller coaster ride.

Remember that rest is not just a physical necessity, but a spiritual one as well. So, don't be afraid to take a break, unwind, and recharge your batteries. After all, even God took a day off after creating the universe—and if it's good enough for Him, it's definitely good enough for us. May you find peace and rest in the loving arms of Jesus, and may your souls be refreshed like never before. Amen!

Chapter 14

Seeking Love in a Hateful World

Introduction: Living in love despite hatred

I N A WORLD FILLED with hatred, violence, and division, it's challenging to live a life of love as a Christian. However, the Bible teaches us that love conquers all, and as followers of Christ, we are called to love one another despite the hatred that surrounds us. So, welcome to the Love Revolution! Even in a world where hate trends, we're diving into how to flip the script and spread love like confetti.

Get ready to explore how we can live in love despite the hatred in our lives and learn to discover the power of God's love and how you can unleash it in your life. John 13:34 drops the mic with Jesus' command: "Love one another. As I have loved you, so you must love one another." It's like God's setting the stage for the ultimate love fest.

And as Christians, we must remember love is at the core of our faith. In 1 John 4:7-8, it tells us that "Beloved, let us love one another, for love is from God, and whoever loves has been born of God and knows God. Anyone who does not love does not know God, because God is love."

This powerful truth reminds us that love is not just a feeling, but a divine attribute that we are called to embody in our daily lives. Despite the challenges we may face, we can find strength and inspiration in the example set by Jesus Christ. Even in the face of betrayal, persecution, and ultimately death on the cross, Jesus showed an unwavering love for all people. His example serves as a beacon of hope for us as we navigate a world filled with hatred and strife.

We can find solace in the promise that love never fails. 1 Corinthians 13:7 tells us that love "bears all things, believes all things, hopes all things, endures all things." By choosing to love others despite the hatred we may encounter, we can find healing and restoration in our pain.

Love extends beyond the confines of personal affection and romantic connections. It encompasses a universal benevolence—a deep-rooted empathy and kindness towards all beings. Such love is radical in its refusal to discriminate, its resilience against cynicism, and its courage in facing hostility. To nurture love is to dismantle barriers of fear, prejudice, and indifference that stifle our shared humanity.

This process begins with self-compassion, or one cannot pour from an empty cup. Embracing our own imperfections allows us to extend grace to others, facilitating a culture of understanding and acceptance. From this foundation, love radiates outward, influencing our interactions, decisions, and, ultimately, the societal frameworks within which we operate.

Ultimately, living in love despite hatred is not just a choice, but a calling for all Christians. As we strive to embody the love of Christ in our daily lives, we can be a shining light in a world that is often consumed by darkness. By seeking biblical guidance and holding fast to the truth that love conquers all, we can live a life filled with purpose, faith, and mental well-being.

Biblical Context: 1 Corinthians 13: Love chapter; 1 John 4:7-8: God is love

Love isn't just a warm fuzzy feeling—it's a significant change. In the Bible, there are many verses that speak about the importance of love in the Christian faith. One of the most well-known passages comes from in 1 Corinthians 13. This chapter eloquently describes the characteristics of love and how it should be the foundation of all our actions and relationships. 1 Corinthians 13:13 reminds us, "And now these three remain: faith, hope and love. But the greatest of these is love."

The 13th chapter of 1 Corinthians, often called the "Love Chapter," is where the apostle Paul beautifully describes the attributes and importance of love. This chapter reminds us that love is patient, kind, does not envy or boast, is not proud or rude, and always perseveres. It is a powerful reminder of the central role that love plays in our lives as Christians.

When we seek to understand the biblical context of love, we remember that love is not just a feeling, but a choice and an action that we must intentionally practice in our daily lives. So, if you ever find yourself in a pickle and don't know how to respond, just remember: love is patient, love is kind, and love never fails. And if all else fails, just bake some cookies for your neighbor—it's a foolproof way to show love!

Another key verse emphasizes the importance of love comes in 1 John 4:7-8, in which we see God is love. This powerful truth reinforces the importance of love in our lives and relationships. As we seek to understand God's character and nature, we see that love is at the core of who He is.

This truth should inspire us to love others as God loves us, unconditionally and sacrificially. When we experience God's love in our lives, we are transformed and empowered to love others in the same way. This verse reminds us love is not just a feeling or an action, but it is at the core of Who God is. So, the next time you're feeling down or unsure of yourself, just remember that God loves you unconditionally. And if that doesn't put a smile on your face, I don't know what will!

The message of love in 1 Corinthians 13 and 1 John 4:7-8 offers hope and guidance. In times of suffering and pain, we can find comfort in knowing God's love doesn't waver. When we struggle with doubts and questions about our faith, we can turn to the truth that God is love and His love never fails. As we seek purpose and calling in our lives, we can trust that love is the foundation upon which we build our lives and relationships.

In times of mental health struggles and emotional turmoil, the message of love in the Bible can bring healing and restoration. When we feel overwhelmed by the challenges of life, we can find strength in knowing that God's love is always with us, guiding and sustaining us. As we navigate the complexities of relationships and conflicts, we can rely on the wisdom of 1 Corinthians 13 to guide our words and actions with love and grace.

Ultimately, the biblical context of love in 1 Corinthians 13 and 1 John 4:7-8 reminds us of the transformative power of love in our lives. Let the truth that God is love and His love never fails inspire us. As you navigate through life's toughest questions, remember to always come back to the foundation of love. Whether you're dealing with difficult relationships, struggles with faith, or just trying to figure out your purpose in life, love should always be your guiding light. May you strive to love others as God loves us, and may we find comfort, strength, and purpose in the unending love of our Heavenly Father.

As Christians, we are called to love one another as Christ loved us. And Christ set the bar pretty high for love. I mean, the guy literally sacrificed himself for the entire world. Talk about commitment! But fear not, for we too can show love in our everyday lives. Whether it's helping a neighbor with their groceries, volunteering at a local shelter, or simply offering a kind word to a stranger, there are countless ways we can emulate Christ's love for others.

Living Out Love

One of the most powerful lessons we can learn is the importance of love. The Bible tells us love is the greatest commandment, and it is through Christ's example that we can truly understand what it means to love others. By following in His footsteps and showing love to those around us, we can make a powerful impact on the world.

One practical application of this principle is loving others through Christ's example. Jesus showed us the ultimate act of love by sacrificing Himself for our sins. In our daily lives, we can strive to emulate His love by showing compassion, forgiveness, and kindness to those we encounter. By doing so, we not only fulfill the commandment to love our neighbors as ourselves, but we also spread the love of Christ to those who may need it most.

Another way we can apply the principle of love is by doing everything in life with love. This means loving God first and above all else, and loving others as ourselves. When we prioritize our relationship with God and seek to love Him with all our heart, soul, and mind, we are better equipped to love others in a genuine and selfless way. By living a life of love, we can reflect God's light to the world and bring hope and healing to those around us.

1. **Receive God's Love:** Picture God handing you a giant heart-shaped box of chocolates—except His love lasts longer than any sweet treat. Embrace it!

2. **Love Others:** Spread love like glitter (minus the mess). Show God's love in how you treat everyone—yes, even that person who double-parks.

3. **Practice Sacrificial Love:** It's not about what's convenient; it's about putting others first. Sacrificial love means giving the last slice of pizza ... even if it has your favorite toppings.

Biblical Examples

Throughout the Bible, we find stories of love that inspire and encourage us on our own journeys. From the beautiful friendship between Ruth and Naomi to Jesus' ultimate act of sacrificial love on the cross, the Bible contains many with examples of love in its purest form. The story of Ruth and Naomi is a beautiful example of sacrificial love between family members. Despite facing hardship and loss, Ruth remained loyal to Naomi, showing her unwavering love and support.

Similarly, Jesus' sacrificial love for us is the ultimate example of love in action. His willingness to die for our salvation reveals the depth and breadth of God's love for each of us.

And last, the Early Church showed true love in the way they lived, making sure everyone was taken care of. So, the next time you're feeling overwhelmed or discouraged, take a moment to reflect on these stories and let them inspire you to love more deeply and fully in your own life. After all, if Ruth and Naomi can stick together through thick and thin, and Jesus can die for our sins out of sheer love, then surely, we can find it in ourselves to show a little love to those around us. Amen to that, am I right?

- **Ruth and Naomi:** Upon the death or Ruth's husband and Naomi's son, Ruth becomes a childless widow who selflessly accompanies her mother-in-law, Naomi, to Judah. She pledges total loyalty, unconditional love, even unto death, to Naomi, her people, and God (1:11–17).

- **Jesus:** Talk about setting the bar high—Jesus showed us what love looks like by sacrificing Himself for us (John 3:16). That's more than just a Hallmark moment!

- **The Early Church:** They weren't just brunch buddies—they lived out love by sharing everything and supporting each other (Acts 2:42-47). It's like the original #SquadGoals.

Practical Application

In doing everything in life with love, it's important to remember to love God first and above all. After all, He is the source of all love and without Him, our love for others would be incomplete. So next time you're facing a tough decision or struggling with a difficult situation, remember to turn to God first and ask for His guidance. And hey, maybe throw in a little "I love you, God" while you're at it. He'll appreciate the sincere sentiment, I'm sure.

And let's not forget about loving others like ourselves. This is tough, especially when faced with people who test our patience or push our buttons. But even Jesus had to deal with some pretty difficult folks (looking at you, Pharisees).

So, take a deep breath, say a quick prayer, and remember to treat others with the same love and respect that you would want for yourself. Who knows, you might just win over that annoying coworker or distant relative with your newfound love-filled attitude. Try these things to sprinkle some love in your daily grind:

1. **Intentional Kindness:** Go beyond holding the door—buy someone's coffee, compliment a stranger, or share your umbrella in a downpour.

2. **Forgiveness:** It's like hitting the reset button on a friendship. Let go of grudges and let grace flow—just like God forgives us.

3. **Community Service:** Roll up your sleeves and get hands on. Whether it's serving meals at a shelter or cleaning up a park, love looks good on you.

Conclusion

Let us remember the power of love in all that we do. By following Christ's example and loving others as He loves us, we can bring light and hope to a world in need. Let us take inspiration from the stories of love in the Bible and strive to live lives filled with love, compassion, and grace. In doing so, we can truly make a difference in the lives of those around us and bring glory to God.

The biblical context of love in 1 Corinthians 13 and 1 John 4:7-8 serves as a reminder to Christian readers that love should be the driving force behind all that we do. So, when faced with a tough question or a challenging situation, just remember to approach it with love in your heart. And if you ever doubt the power of love, just remember God is love, and His love never fails.

And remember, in a world that could use a love makeover, you've already got the tools. By receiving God's love, loving others, and practicing sacrificial love, you're not just making waves—you're changing the tide. So, grab your love cape (yes, it's a thing) and remember 1 Corinthians 13:13: "But the greatest of these is love."

Let's make the world a better place—one loving gesture at a time! Go forth with confidence, knowing that God loves you beyond measure and that love will always prevail in the end.

Chapter 15

Seeking The Divine in a Godless World

Introduction: Connecting with the divine in a secular world

T HROUGHOUT THE HISTORY OF humanity, we've searched for something to fill the God-shaped hole in our lives in every way and form, usually in the wrong places. We've searched for the elusive fountain of youth, to live forever, and to implement self-salvation. However, deep down, in its core, the human quest for eternity or salvation is not merely a pursuit of immortality, but a deep desire to be in everlasting harmony with the Divine—that is, to return to the Source of all beings. It is a journey that involves reflection, repentance, and transformation—a spiritual evolution that aligns one's life with the principles and virtues that are believed to lead to eternal life.

Interestingly enough, however, Isaiah 55:6 says to "Seek the Lord while He may be found; and call on Him while He is near." So, welcome to the ultimate treasure hunt—finding God in a world that sometimes feels like He's playing hide and seek. Tuning in to His presence and experiencing the divine firsthand feels almost impossible with all the noise. In fact, in a secular world that often seems to prioritize materialism and individualism, it's challenging to maintain a strong connection with the divine.

For Christians, it is essential to remember that our faith can provide us with guidance and support even in the most secular of environments. By prioritizing our relationship with God and seeking His wisdom in all aspects of our lives, we can find peace and purpose in a world that often seems chaotic and overwhelming.

In today's fast-paced, secular world, connecting with the divine can feel like a daunting task. With constant distractions and the hustle and bustle of daily life, it's easy to sideline our spiritual needs. Yet nurturing our relationship with God is crucial for our well-being and sense of purpose. The Bible encourages us to seek God intentionally. Isaiah 55:6 reminds us that the Lord is always near, waiting for us to reach out to Him.

Biblical Context: Acts 17:27: God is close to all of us; Psalm 42:1: Thirsting for God

Acts 17:27 reminds us God is not playing hide and seek with us and that He is close to all of us. He's not some elusive deity hiding behind a cloud or playing peek-a-boo in the bushes. No, God is actually pretty close by. In fact, he's so close that he's practically breathing down our necks (in a non-creepy way, of course). So, next time you're feeling lost or alone, just remember that God is right there with you, probably rolling his eyes at your dramatics.

This powerful verse serves as a comforting assurance that, no matter where we are in life, God is always nearby. We can take solace because we are never alone. God's presence is always with us, guiding us through the challenges and triumphs of life.

Now, let's talk about Psalm 42:1, where the psalmist declares that his soul thirsts for God, having a deep longing for Him. Now, I don't know about you, but when I'm thirsty, I usually reach for a nice cool glass of water or maybe a refreshing lemonade. But this guy? He's not looking for a beverage, he's looking for the Almighty Creator of the Universe. Talk about high standards! I mean, I get it. We all want to quench our spiritual thirst, but maybe a nice cup of tea would suffice? Of course not.

In fact, as the psalmist states, just as a deer pants for streams of water, our own souls also thirst for the Lord's presence. This verse reminds us of our innate desire to be in communion with God, seeking His love, comfort, and guidance. As we navigate the complexities of life, it is essential to remember that our ultimate fulfillment can only be found in our relationship with Him.

Acts 17:27 and Psalm 42:1 serve as powerful reminders that God is always near, even in our darkest moments. By turning to Him and seeking His comfort, we can find solace in our struggles. Our purpose and calling in life connect to our relationship with God. And just as a deer yearns for water, our souls long for His presence, guidance, and direction. By seeking God in all that we do, we can align our lives with His will and fulfill the unique calling He has placed on each of us. As we meditate on Acts 17:27 and Psalm 42:1, let us remember that our ultimate purpose is to seek God and His kingdom above all else.

We can take comfort because God is always close by, even when we feel like he's MIA. And when we're feeling spiritually parched, we can seek God to satisfy our thirst for meaning and purpose. The next time you find yourself in a tough spot or grappling with life's big questions, remember these verses. God is not far off, and He's always ready to quench your spiritual thirst. And who knows, maybe he'll even bring along a snack. After all, man does not live on bread alone, right? So, keep seeking and keep thirsting.

Seeking God

In a world that often pulls us away from our spiritual roots, making intentional efforts to connect with God keeps us anchored. It renews our spirit, gives us peace, and helps us navigate life with a sense of purpose and fulfillment. And one of the most powerful ways to deepen our relationship with God is through prayer and worship. Prayer allows us to communicate with God, sharing our hopes, fears, and dreams with Him.

It is a way to open our hearts to Him and invite His presence into our lives. Similarly, worship is a way to honor God for who He is and what He has done for us. By taking the time to pray and worship regularly, we can strengthen our connection with God and experience His love in a deeper way.

When we have God in our lives, we have a purpose and a hope that transcends the trials and tribulations of this world. Knowing that our Creator love and value us gives us a sense of worth and meaning that cannot be found elsewhere. With God in our lives, we can face each day with confidence, knowing that He is with us every step of the way. Life with God is truly worth living, as He fills our hearts with joy and peace that surpasses all understanding.

1. **Wholehearted Pursuit:** Imagine seeking God like you're on a mission to find the last slice of pizza at a party—wholehearted and determined!

2. **Persistent Prayer:** Think of persistent prayer like texting your bestie for updates on that Netflix series—you keep asking until you get the spoilers!

3. **Seek God in Scripture:** It's like reading the ultimate life manual to understand the Author's mind and heart. Spoiler alert: God's character and plans are all revealed there.

Biblical Examples

The Bible holds many stories of divine encounters that serve as powerful examples of God's presence and power in our lives. Let's look at some examples of divine encounters in the Bible to see just how powerful a relationship with God can be.

One such example is Moses' encounter with God at the burning bush, where he was called to lead the Israelites out of Egypt. Remember when he encountered the burning bush? Talk about a "hot" conversation starter! Despite his doubts and fears, Moses trusted in God and followed His guidance, ultimately fulfilling his purpose and bringing freedom to his people.

Another good example is that of Enoch's. It is said that he walked with God each day. The word walk entails fellowship with, closeness with, and obedience to God. It refers to the manner of life a person living in closeness to God. Enoch means dedicated, and he dedicated to living daily with God.

One more powerful example is the dramatic conversion of Paul, formerly known as Saul, who was a persecutor of Christians before encountering Jesus on the road to Damascus. Through this divine encounter, Paul's life transformed, and he became one of the greatest apostles in Christian history. If God can transform a persecutor into a preacher, imagine what He can do for you.

These stories remind us that God is always at work in our lives, guiding us and transforming us for His glory. So, next time you're feeling lost or confused, just remember that God has a plan for you, even if it involves a burning bush, a long walk, or a blinding light.

- **Moses:** He didn't just get a phone call from God—he had front-row seats to the divine glory show (Exodus 33:11-23). Burning bush, parting seas—Moses saw it all!

- **Enoch:** This guy was like the OG BFF with God, walking faithfully and experiencing His presence so deeply that he skipped straight to heaven (Genesis 5:24). Talk about life goals!

- **Paul:** His encounter with Jesus on the road to Damascus (Acts 9:1-19; 22:6-21; and 26:12-18) was so life-changing that not only did he change his name, but his entire life's mission changed. And thanks to all his mission trips and preaching, we are here today!

Practical Application

Imagine God as your best friend Who's always there to listen to your rants, your praises, and even your bad jokes. Just like any relationship, communication is key. So, talk to God, sing to God, dance for God (if you're feeling brave). Remember, God loves you just the way you are, quirks, and all. Understanding that with God in our lives, life is worth living can be a game-changer.

Think of God as the ultimate life coach, guiding you through the challenges, twists, and turns. When you have God on your team, suddenly those Monday mornings don't seem so daunting, and that pile of laundry doesn't seem so overwhelming. With God, every day is a new adventure, full of surprises and blessings. Here's how to dial up your divine connection:

1. **Daily Devotion:** Set aside time daily—like your morning coffee ritual—but with God. Prayer and Bible study brew up spiritual caffeine! Remember, connecting with God doesn't have to be structured religious activities. Carve out moments daily to look for Him in nature, in your daily interactions, and in the simple joys of life. Use this time to listen, reflect, and draw closer to Him.

2. **Community Worship:** It's like a spiritual pep rally! Join in worship and fellowship with others who are on this divine quest too. Being part of a church or small group can provide support and encouragement. Sharing your journey with others who seek God can deepen your faith and offer mutual accountability.

3. **Spiritual Disciplines:** Think of them as your workout routine for the soul—intentionally engaging in Scripture, practicing gratitude, worshiping and praising through music, fasting, meditation, and other disciplines that flex your spiritual muscles. Regularly practicing helps you stay grounded in His truth and provides guidance for your life, while it also shifts your focus from the secular distractions to His continuous presence and provision.

Conclusion

God is not hiding. He is ever available and ready to be in relationship with us. In fact, not only does He welcome us to seek Him, but He encourages us to do so. And while for some of us, seeking the Divine might have challenges by moments of doubt, uncertainty, or despair, the quest itself and the guide given—the Bible—illuminates our path, guiding us towards a deeper understanding of ourselves, of the world, and of course, the Divine.

But there's another way to enter a relationship with the divine. Deepening our relationship with God through prayer and worship, understanding that life is worth living with God, and reflecting on divine encounters in the Bible can inspire and encourage us. By staying connected to God and trusting in His plan for our lives, we can find hope, purpose, and peace in life's challenges.

In a world where Netflix binges and social media can distract us from the divine, seeking God takes intentionality and persistence. By diving into prayer, delving into Scripture, and practicing spiritual disciplines, you'll uncover God's presence and reality. Remember Jeremiah 29:13: "You will seek me and find me when you seek me with all your heart."

So, grab your spiritual magnifying glass—it's time for a divine adventure! May we seek Him with all our hearts and have a relationship with Him, as Moses, Enoch, and Paul had. May we find our strength, peace, and purpose in our relationship with God, and may He guide us to prioritize our time with Him and to recognize His hand in every aspect of our lives.

As you navigate life's toughest questions, remember that with God by your side, anything is possible. So, go ahead, deepen your relationship with God through prayer and worship, and watch as your life transforms into a beautiful, and ultimately fulfilling, adventure. And who knows, maybe one day you'll have your own divine encounter to share with the world.

Chapter 16

Epilogue: The Journey of Seeking

Reflecting on the Journey

W E HAVE EMBARKED ON quite the adventure together in our quest to seeking and finding answers, and we have delved deep into the pages of the Bible to find wisdom and guidance. And, well, congratulations! You've made it through a whirlwind tour of tough questions, armed with biblical wisdom. From justice to joy, mercy to fulfillment, you've delved deep into God's Word and emerged wiser and more inspired.

It has been a wild ride of twists and turns, but we have come out the other side with a newfound sense of clarity and purpose. Each chapter wasn't just a pit stop but a roadmap, guiding you through the twists and turns of a life lived seeking God's truth. Remember, it's not just about finding answers—it's about the journey itself.

As you come to the end of this book, it is important to reflect on the wisdom and insights that you have gained along the way. From exploring the depths of suffering and pain to uncovering our purpose and calling, you have delved into the Word of God to find the answers you seek. Through faith and doubt, mental health struggles, and moments of clarity, you have discovered that the Bible holds the key to navigating life's challenges with grace and resilience.

In your quest for understanding, you have learned that God is always present, offering comfort and guidance in times of need. And as you continue to seek, you are never alone in our struggles.

Now that we have made it this far, let me offer you some words of encouragement: Keep seeking God with all your heart. The journey doesn't end here—in fact, it's just the beginning. The Bible is a treasure trove of wisdom and insight, and the more you delve into its pages, the more you will uncover. So, keep pressing forward, keep asking tough questions, and keep seeking God with all your heart. Who knows what revelations might wait for you just around the corner?

And as you continue to seek biblical answers to your struggles, take comfort in the knowledge God's love is a constant source of strength and healing. Remember that the Bible is a timeless source of wisdom and truth. By turning to God's Word for guidance and inspiration, you can navigate life's challenges with courage and faith. May you continue to seek His presence in all that you do, knowing that He is the ultimate guide in your quest for understanding and peace.

Continual Seeking

In times of uncertainty and despair, it's easy to lose sight of our faith and question whether God is truly present in our lives. However, He promises to never leave nor forsake us. The journey of seeking biblical answers to life's toughest questions may be challenging, but the rewards of a deeper relationship with God far outweigh any struggles we may face.

When we face doubts or difficulties in life, it can be tempting to turn away from God and question His goodness. But I encourage you to persevere in seeking Him, for He is our source of comfort and strength in times of trouble.

The Bible is full of stories of God's faithfulness to His people in uncertainty, and we can find hope and encouragement in these accounts as we continue to seek Him with all our hearts. So, do not let doubts or fears hinder you, but turn to God in prayer and seek His wisdom and guidance in all things. And in your journey of seeking, keep in mind these three things:

1. **Lifelong Pursuit:** Like trying to find the perfect pair of socks that never disappear in the laundry, seeking God is a lifelong pursuit. Keep searching, keep asking, and keep growing.

2. **Community Support:** Surround yourself with a squad of fellow seekers—think of them as your spiritual entourage. They'll cheer you on when you're tired of asking Google for answers.

3. **Trust in God's Faithfulness:** Just like your favorite delivery app that always brings your order hot and on time, trust that God's faithfulness is unmatched. He'll guide you through every challenge, big or small.

Growth Through Scripture

As we draw this exploration to a close, having traversed the expansive terrains of biblical wisdom to uncover answers to some of life's most perplexing questions, it becomes plain that Scripture does not merely offer a set of answers, but provides a profound understanding and a pathway for navigating life's complexities.

From the poignant reflections on suffering and God's role as depicted in the stories of Genesis, Job, and Ruth, through the heartening accounts of David, Daniel, Paul, and Jesus, which teach us how to endure personal trials with unwavering faith, to the discerning insights into God's will and the essence of making righteous decisions, this journey through biblical narratives has been both enlightening and transforming.

Remember, the Bible is not just a book of stories and rules—it is a powerful tool for strengthening our faith. The verses within its pages have the power to uplift us in times of trouble, to guide us in moments of uncertainty, and to bring us peace when our we struggle. So don't just read the Bible—let it sink into your soul, let it shape your thoughts and actions, and let it strengthen your faith in ways you never thought possible.

Remember Psalm 119:105—"Your word is a lamp to my feet and a light to my path." Let this verse remind you that the Bible is not just a book of words, but a guiding light that can lead you through even the darkest of times.

Strengthening your faith through Scripture is a powerful and transformative practice that all Christian readers should engage in regularly. The Bible is the Living Word of God that has the power to renew our minds, transform our hearts, and guide us through life's toughest questions. By immersing ourselves in Scripture, we can deepen our faith and develop a stronger relationship with God.

When we face suffering and pain in our lives, turning to Scripture can provide comfort, guidance, and hope. The stories of Job, Joseph, and Jesus remind us even in our darkest moments, God is with us, working all things together for our good. By meditating on passages like Romans 8:28, we can find peace in knowing that God is in control and that our suffering has a purpose.

Finding our purpose and calling in life can be a daunting task, but Scripture provides us with clear guidance on how to live a life that is pleasing to God. By studying verses like Jeremiah 29:11 and Ephesians 2:10, we can discover our specific purpose and that God has a plan for our lives. When we align our goals and ambitions with God's will, we can live a fulfilling and purpose-driven life.

In moments of doubt and wavering faith, turning to Scripture can provide us with the strength and reassurance we need to keep. The stories of Abraham, Moses, and David remind us that even the most faithful followers of God experienced moments of doubt and uncertainty. By studying passages like Hebrews 11:1 and Mark 9:24, we can find the courage to trust in God's promises and believe that He will never leave us nor forsake us.

Taking care of our mental health and wellbeing is essential for living a balanced and fulfilling life. By meditating on verses like Philippians 4:6-7 and Psalm 23:4, we can find comfort, peace, and strength in God's presence.

The Bible offers us wisdom and guidance on how to overcome anxiety, depression, and other mental health challenges, reminding us that God is our refuge and strength in times of trouble. By strengthening our faith through Scripture, we can find the peace and joy that surpasses all understanding.

Conclusion

We have ventured into the realms of mercy, hope, love, and the Divine, gleaning from the teachings of Jesus and the profound realizations of divine revelation, recognizing that every snippet of Scripture—from the stories to its characters—is a guide meant to inspire and sustain us through the vicissitudes of life.

It is this realization that allows us to comprehend that seeking answers in Bible is not a quest for mere knowledge, but a journey of faith—a journey that draws us closer to God, shapes our character so that we can live in Kingdom now, and also prepares us for the ultimate destiny that awaits us. Thus, as we anchor ourselves in faith, it is imperative to remember that the journey does not end here.

As we reaffirm our belief in these guiding Bible verses and their promises, let us hold fast to the truth that God is with us in every moment of our lives. May we find strength, comfort, and hope in His word, knowing that He is faithful to fulfill His promises to us. Let us remember that seeking God with all our hearts is a transformative and life-changing journey.

So, your journey of seeking isn't ending here; it's just getting started. Now, armed with biblical wisdom and a heart full of faith, go forth and seek God with all your heart. His presence, guidance, and blessings await you at every turn.

Let us embrace the insights and promises revealed through Scripture with an open heart. May we continue to seek, to question, and to grow, fortified by the conviction that in God, we find not only the answers to our deepest questions but also the assurance of His unfailing love and the hope of eternal life.

And finally, let's take a moment to reaffirm the guiding Bible verses that have led us on this journey. And as we meditate on the guiding verses of Jeremiah 29:13, Matthew 7:7, and Amos 5:17, may we have the courage to seek after God's truth, goodness, and presence with unwavering faith and dedication. May our seeking lead us to a deeper understanding of God's will for our lives and a closer walk with Him in all that we do.

- Jeremiah 29:13: "You will seek me and find me when you seek me with all your heart." Think of it as the ultimate treasure hunt with eternal rewards.

- Matthew 7:7: "Ask and it will be given to you; seek and you will find; knock and the door will be opened to you." It's like having a VIP pass to God's wisdom and blessings.

- Amos 5:17: Okay, this one's a bit of a mood shift, but it reminds us to seek good and not evil—to make choices that reflect God's heart.

Seek God with all your heart, and you will find Him experiencing His presence, guidance, and blessings in every aspect of your life. Happy seeking!

Acknowledgments

F IRST AND FOREMOST, I want to give a huge shoutout to God to express my deepest gratitude. Seriously, where would we be without His wisdom and guidance? Lost in the parking lot, that's probably where! So, thankyou, Lord, for always knowing the way and for those little nudges in the right direction when I tried to take a U-turn. Your wisdom and guidance have been the cornerstone of this book, and without Your divine insight, unending grace, and constant source of inspiration, this work would not have been possible. To You be all the glory and honor.

To my amazing, beloved wife, the rock of my salvation (no wait, that's Jesus!), my better half, my compass when I'm hopelessly lost: your continual support has been nothing short of miraculous. You've listened to my ramblings, endured my writer's block-induced mood swings, and still managed to smile through it all. Your unwavering support and constant belief in me have been my strength and fuel throughout this journey. I couldn't have done this without your love and patience. And yes, I promise to finally take out the bathroom trash... but only if you promise to put away your clothes.

A big thank you to my family and friends. Your encouragement has been the wind beneath my wings, or maybe the caffeine in my coffee that I don't drink. Either way, I'm grateful. You've provided wisdom, constructive criticism (and some not-so-constructive),and plenty of laughs along the way. You've kept me grounded and reminded me to take breaks and breathe. But seriously, your encouragement, wisdom, insights, feedback, and prayers have been invaluable. I appreciate all of you.

Lastly, to you, dear readers, whoever you are, thank you for joining me on this adventure of seeking. Your willingness to dive into this book and embark on this journey of seeking together is like finding a kindred spirit who also finds joy in the quirky and profound. I hope this book brings you as many insights (and some chuckles) as I had writing it. Remember, we're all seeking together—sometimes stumbling, sometimes soaring, but always learning and growing, and always marching forward. It is my hope that this book serves as a beacon of light and hope in your quest for deeper understanding and connection with the divine. Thank you for allowing me to be a part of your spiritual journey.

About the Author

O BED OLIVARRÍA WAS BORN in Mexicali, Mexico and spent his youth as a fully bicultural transnational citizen. He has a passion for writing both fiction and nonfiction, public speaking, composing, arranging, and performing mostly jazz music, as well as traveling around the world. He loves the thrill of adrenaline-pumping activities, but also the quiet reflection he gets from writing and creating.

Obed has worked as a youth and young adult pastor, as a freelance graphic designer, as a session musician, as a ministry consultant, and as university dean. Having worked at every level of the education system, from pre-k to university, has given him an expedition to the human psyche. He has a dynamic love of life and ministry, and he is a deep thinker, and an honest intellectual to the Gospel of Jesus.

Obed lives in sunny Orange County, California with his charming wife and two energetic children, where he works as a school psychologist by day. In the future, Obed hopes to be able to continue to write inspiring books that entertain, but also challenge the status quo. On a personal level, he would like to visit every country in the world, perhaps drawing inspiration from these travels for another great story.

www.ingramcontent.com/pod-product-compliance
Lightning Source LLC
Chambersburg PA
CBHW071533120626
46550CB00006B/2439